I0814703

MIRROR
镜中

Poems by

Zhang Zao
张枣

Translated from Chinese by Fiona Sze-Lorrain
with an Afterword by Bei Dao

Zephyr Press

Cover image by Xu Bing
Book design by typeslowly
Printed in Michigan by Cushing-Malloy

This publication is supported by the Jintian Literary Foundation.
Zephyr Press also acknowledges with gratitude the financial support
of the Massachusetts Cultural Council and the Academy of American Poets
with funds from the Amazon Literary Partnership Poetry Fund.

Zephyr Press, a nonprofit arts and education 501(c)(3) organization,
publishes literary titles that foster a deeper understanding of cultures
and languages. Zephyr Press books are distributed to the trade in the U.S.
and Canada by Consortium Book Sales and Distribution [www.cbsd.com].

Cataloguing-in-publication data is available from the Library of Congress.

ZEPHYR PRESS
www.zephyrpress.org

JINTIAN
www.jintian.net

CONTENTS

After an Epic Voice

Mirror: Selected Poems by Zhang Zao marks the first time I have translated a selection of poems chosen to collectively represent the oeuvre of a non-living Chinese contemporary poet. Because of Zhang's death in 2010, his poems suddenly became final and complete—*set in stone*, as they say—even though we poets, writers, translators—and readers—know that words never cease to revise their own meaning through time and interpretation. Translating Zhang Zao's work taught me the importance of taking these future meanings—the foreign, the unknown, the unsaid—into account. I learned to do so by interacting with his poems in different, sometimes conflicting, time spaces. I brought myself to read Zhang Zao the way I would read Victor Hugo or Theodectes. There is an epic voice in his verses. But rather than imitating the greats, our poet has created a polyphonic texture with an innovative feel and esoteric imagery. There is jazz. There is traditional opera. Then the folk music. And the electric. Although his style is eclectic, flamboyant, at times unpredictable, Zhang's writing is rooted in formal structure. Every poem is an experimentation with the form and line—not one is alike. And its lyricism fuels Zhang Zao's ambition for the narrative to embed speculative allegory, literary sources, and historical references within the experience of a contemporary exile.

Books and media today describe Zhang Zao as a key literary figure of the "third generation" of Chinese contemporary poetry. Born on December 29, 1962 in Changsha, Hunan province, Zhang came from a cultured family. His father was a teacher in Russian and Chinese, and an accomplished calligrapher. Zhang Zao enrolled in Hunan Normal School in 1978, majoring in English. Already a prodigy, he was barely sixteen when he began college. Zhang taught briefly after graduation. In 1983, he moved to Sichuan, where he forged new literary friendships, renewing his poetic faith and inspiration. Soon he rose to national fame as one of the "Five Sichuan Masters." In his company were four other poets: Zhong Ming (b. 1953), Zhai Yongming (b. 1955), Bai Hua (b. 1956), and Ouyang Jianghe (b. 1956).

At twenty-two, Zhang Zao found immediate acclaim for his twelve-line poem "Mirror." But as a growing poet and the youngest of his group, Zhang did not seem interested in the "easy" route, where he could produce—and reproduce—the same kind of "work that works." He was keen on composing difficult sequence lyrics and long dramatic monologues, which was unusual among his peers and would later become a characteristic aspect of his poetic expression.

Greatly admired for his ability to champion a complex yet harmonizing fusion of traditional writing and avant-garde flair in his own poetry, Zhang Zao was versatile in not just one or two but several foreign languages. He was proficient in English, German, French, and Russian. In addition, he was able to read Latin. This too was uncommon among Chinese poets at that time. Although he had confessed his reluctance about translation, stating that it was impossible to translate poetry, Zhang in time accepted requests to translate the work of Paul Celan, Georg Trakl, René Char, Mark Strand, Seamus Heaney, as well as a significant portion of Wallace Stevens's writings. Later, with the translator Chen Dongbiao, he compiled his translations of Stevens into a book-length volume, published by East China Normal University Press in 2009 and reissued in a new edition in 2021. Zhang also translated an essay by Rilke and another by C. G. Jung, as well as fiction by contemporary German illustrator and storyteller Einar Turkowski (*Moon Flowers* and *Cloud-fishing*) and American writer Pamela Hennell ("Great Grandma's Book").

Zhang was viewed as an intellectual poet in part due to his work in academia. His research involved literary criticism, translation, and philosophy. As a scholar, he lectured and wrote both in German and Chinese on subjects ranging from Lu Xun to Eliot and Yeats to Gennady Aygi. He was also involved in the editorial work for a bilingual German-Chinese/Chinese-German dictionary, published in 2008. Back in 1986, Zhang Zao married a German teacher based in Sichuan. The couple moved to Germany, where they set up residence and Zhang pursued his graduate studies, but their marriage did not last. Zhang Zao stayed on in Germany, earning a doctorate in literature and philosophy from the University of Tübingen in 1994. For several years, he served as poetry editor for the literary magazine *Jintian* and taught at the University of Tübingen. After much deliberation, Zhang Zao returned briefly to China in 2004 and taught a semester at Henan University the next spring. In 2007, he was appointed a professor at the Minzu University of China. Toward the end of 2009, he abruptly fell ill and after being diagnosed with lung cancer in Beijing, Zhang returned to Germany for medical treatment. He died on March 7, 2010 in Tübingen, the town of Hölderlin. He was forty-seven.

In a local newspaper of Tübingen, Zhang Zao's obituary includes an excerpt from his sequence of sonnets "Dialogue with Tsvetaeva," written sixteen years before the poet's untimely death:

> a word is not an object—this must be made clear,
> so one must first live an interesting life
> like at this instant—lush magnolia blooms stand on their own, pouring
> out their woes.
> The siren stops like a lover's hair floating to the ground.

Live an interesting life: indeed, Zhang was fascinated not just by language but by life itself. He was acutely aware of his comfort zone in a university town and yearned for more social reach. During my research, I've found out from his friends and colleagues that our poet was a gourmand and wine lover. As a person he was very much an epicurean: indulgent, pleasure-seeking, unrestrained. Instead of melancholia, Zhang Zao's work tends more toward exuberance and expansion. As a philosopher and critic, the poet practices reflective judgment in his own aesthetics. Dark humor vivifies his later imagination as he eroticizes the harrowing, the liminal, the imminent: doubt, absence, finality, and nothingness. Both volitional and temporal asymmetries—in what we may call a poetic line—enact possibilities in which a nonsimultaneity of events, happenings, actions, scenes, and conversations summons us first to listening, then witnessing and recording.

The choice of poems in this volume is retrospective, though short of summary: the opening poem "Mirror" is one of Zhang Zao's earliest and also his best-known work; "Lantern Town"—written less than two months before his death—is his last. Evoking his adopted home and the impossibility of exile, the music in his farewell piece is performed a cappella in two parts, built on silence, struggling whispers, chants, and echoes. Like the sonic architecture of a near-death experience, where lucidity meets pain with utter honesty, the poem is to me reminiscent of the speechlessness and austerity in Beckett's last work, "what is the word" (*Comment dire*, 1988).

I started working on this translation in December 2011. But I never imagined the road to its publication would take more than twelve years. Despite the time I have spent living with Zhang Zao's work, I still find something in it that eludes my comprehension, defies any explanation. In short, these poems can be strange. But the dialogue continues. Past the point of frustration, I have learned to accept my limits as translator and for that matter, I have no intent in presenting myself as a specialist of any author I translate. Some of these verses remain a riddle, others like old wine taking on a new taste. The missing piece is what makes the puzzle compelling.

As I dig into my final version of these poems, I can't help but feel a sense of joy and relief. My favorites include "The Prince of Chu Dreams of Rain," "Schermanski the German Soldier's Death Sentence," "Dialogue with Tsvetaeva," "Nightview, New York," "Chef," "Letter in Four Seasons," "Earth Song," "In the Pacific Ocean, a Small Island Nation" . . . The list goes on. Since his death, Zhang's work has experienced a remarkable surge in interest in mainland China. His collection *Poems by Zhang Zao* was published by People's Literature Publishing House in July 2010. Reprinted many times in three editions, it has sold over sixty thousand copies and been included in numerous lists for best poetry titles. Other posthumous publications followed. More recently, after the tenth anniversary of Zhang's passing, a five-volume box set titled *Collected Poetry and Prose of Zhang Zao* appeared in March 2021 from Sichuan Literature and Art Publishing House. Comprising Zhang's collected poems, dissertation, essays, lectures, correspondence, interviews, and translations, the box set has gone into two reprints and sold at least eleven thousand copies.

Notwithstanding the uncountable nonofficial reproduction of Zhang's writings during his lifetime, the current sales figures of *Poems by Zhang Zao* and *Collected Poetry and Prose of Zhang Zao* represent only a fraction of the poet's cultural and artistic influence. Both the collection and the five-volume compilation were edited by Yan Lianjun, one of Zhang Zao's former students and now the literary executor of his estate. In response to my question about the ongoing reception of Zhang's work in mainland China, Yan informs me that Zhang Zao's readership consists of predominantly young readers, which he deems an "interesting phenomenon." The poem "Mirror" also inspired several pop singers, including Lao Lang (Old Wolf) and Zhou Yunpeng, who have adapted or set it to music and recorded and performed their versions to notable success.

Zhang Zao's *Mirror: Selected Poems* concludes the line of bilingual poetry titles in the Jintian series. Several of these translations first appeared in their different forms in *The Antigonish Review, The Antioch Review, Grain, Mānoa, Mantis, Modern Poetry in Translation, New Humanist, Ninth Letter, POEM, Poetry London, Two Lines,* and *West Branch*. During the early stages of this project, Bai Hua offered suggestions for the choice of selection and responded to my questions. Christina Cook, Jan Wagner, Olivier Schwartz from Contours Soft Design in Paris, and Richard Jandovitz from the Columbia University C.V. Starr East Asian Library also helped me along the way. Christopher Mattison edited the book. I fact-checked sources and proofread the original texts with Yan Lianjun. Any error or omission is otherwise mine. I hope it too can be creative.

Fiona Sze-Lorrain
Paris, August 2024

Manuscript of Zhang Zao's "Mirror,"
Autumn 1984

重庆钢铁工业学校公用笺

镜中

只要想起一生中后悔的事
梅花便落了下来
比如游泳到河的另一岸
比如看见的雪片
危险的事固然美丽，不如
羞惭，低下头，回答着皇帝
看她骑马归来
一面镜子永远等候她
让她坐在镜中常坐的地方
望着窗外，想起一生中后悔的事
梅花便落满了南山

地址：重庆市杨家坪　　电话：23572

镜中

只要想起一生中后悔的事
梅花便落了下来
比如看她游泳到河的另一岸
比如登上一株松木梯子
危险的事固然美丽
不如看她骑马归来
面颊温暖，
羞惭。低下头，回答着皇帝
一面镜子永远等候她
让她坐到镜中常坐的地方
望着窗外，只要想起一生中后悔的事
梅花便落满了南山

Mirror

Once regrets come to mind
plum blossoms fall
Like watching her swim to the other shore
Like climbing a pine ladder
Beauty exists in danger
Why not watch her return on horseback
cheeks warm
with shame. Head bowed, she answers the Emperor
A mirror awaits her forever
Let her take her usual place in the mirror
Looking out the window, once regrets come to mind
plum blossoms fall over the southern mountain

何人斯

究竟那是什么人？在外面的声音
只可能在外面。你的心地幽深莫测
青苔的井边有棵铁树。进了门
为何你不来找我，只是溜向
悬满干鱼的木梁下，我们曾经
一同结网，你钟爱过跟水波说话的我
你此刻追踪的是什么？
为何对我如此暴虐

我们有时也背靠着背，韶华流水
我抚平你额上的皱纹，手掌因编织
而温暖；你和我本来是一件东西
享受另一件东西：纸窗、星宿和锅
谁使眼睛昏花
一片雪花转为两片雪花
鲜鱼开了膛，血腥淋漓；你进了门
为何不来问寒问暖
冷冰冰地溜动，门外的山丘缄默

这是我钟情的第十个月
我的光阴嫁给了一个影子
我咬一口自己摘来的鲜桃，让你
清洁的牙齿也尝一口；甜润得
让你也全身膨胀如感激
为何只有你说话的声音
不见你遗留的晚餐皮果
空空的外衣留着灰垢

Who Art Thou

Who on earth is that? The voice outside
can only stay outside. Your heart is unfathomable
A cycad grows by the mossy well. Why didn't you look
for me when you came in, but instead slipped under
a wooden beam hung with dried fish? We once
wove a net together, you once loved me who talks to ripples
What are you pursuing now?
Why are you so cruel to me—

Sometimes we face each other back to back, glorious youth
like flowing water
I smooth the wrinkles on your forehead, palms warm
from weaving; you and I were one thing
enjoying another: paper windows, constellations, woks
Who drives our eyes bleary?
A fleck of snow twisted into two
Fresh fish with open chests, dripping with blood; why didn't you ask
how things were going when you came in
gliding around coldly, reserved hills outside the door

This is my tenth month of love
My time is wed to a shadow
I take a bite of fresh peach I plucked, let your
clean teeth taste, so mellow and sweet
your whole body expands gratefully
Why is there only your speaking voice?
Leftover fruit peels of your dinner nowhere to be seen
with soot remaining on the empty coat

不见你的脸，香烟袅袅上升
　　你没有脸对人，对我？

究竟那是什么人？一切变迁
皆从手指开始。伐木丁丁，想起
你的那些姿势，一个风暴便灌满了楼阁
疾风紧张而突兀
不在北边也不在南边
我们的甬道冷得酸心刺骨

你要是正缓缓向前行进
马匹悠懒，六根辔绳积满阴天
你要是正匆匆向前行进
马匹婉转，长鞭飞扬

二月开白花，你逃也逃不脱，你在哪儿休息
哪儿就被我守望着。你若告诉我
你的双臂怎样垂落，我就会告诉你
你将怎样再一次招手；你若告诉我
你看见什么东西正在消逝
我就会告诉你，你是哪一个

1984

Your face nowhere, tobacco smoke curling
            Have you no cheek to face the others and me?

Who on earth is that? Everything is in flux
beginning with the fingers. Clinks and clangs. As I recall
your postures, a storm fills up the pavilion
A nervous, lofty gale
neither in the north nor the south
Our passageway is despairingly cold

Should you advance with ease
languid horses, six reins stuffed with an overcast sky
Should you advance in haste
tactful horses, swishing whips

White flowers blossom in February: you can't flee, wherever you rest
I'll be on guard. If you tell me
how your arms slump, I'll tell you
how you'd wave again; if you tell me
what you see vanishing
I'll tell you which one you are

1984

秋天的戏剧

1

去秋我把他们写得芬芳清晰
守在某棵月桂下，各司其职
他们没有哪点冷落过我，也依稀
听闻过我的名姓，我依恋过
其中的某些面孔，对于别些个
他们的怯懦和不幸，我也多少抱有怜悯
今年这时节落叶纷纷，回头四顾
泥泞的道上又新添了几场霏雨

2

我潜心做着语言的试验
一遍又一遍地，我默念着誓言
我让冲突发生在体内的节奏中
睫毛与嘴角最小的蠕动，可以代替
从前的利剑和一次钟情，主角在一个地方
可以一步不挪，或者偶尔出没
我便赋予其真实的声响和空气的震动
变凉的物体间，让他们加厚衣襟，痛定思痛

3

他们改不了这样或那样的习惯
而我甚是苛求，其实我也知道孰能无过
念错一句热爱的话语又算什么?
只是习惯太深，他们甚至不会打量别人
秋声簌簌，更不会为别人的幸福而打动

Autumn Drama

1

Last autumn, I described them as fragrant and clear
under a laurel tree, each to his own work
They'd never neglected me, vaguely
knew my name; I once loved
some of these faces, as for the others
their cowardice and mishaps, I more or less sympathized
Leaves fall this year in this season, turn and look around
New drizzle along the muddy way

2

I delve into language trials
Again and again, I silently recite my pledge
let clashes happen in bodily rhythm
The slightest squirm of eyelashes and lip corners replaces
a sharp sword from the past and a love. The protagonist
doesn't need to take a step, or from time to time when he appears
I'll confer upon him authentic sounds and jarring air
Between cooled things, people put on more clothes, learn from their
bitter past

3

They can't kick this or that habit
Yet I keep demanding, knowing that to err is human
Who cares if a phrase much loved is read wrongly?
As long as their habits are old they can't size each other up
much less moved by others' bliss in this autumn rustle

为别人的泪花儿奔赴约会。我不能
怎么也不能改变他们；明镜的孤独中
他们的固执成了我深深的梦寐

4

那一个，那幼稚母亲的掌上明珠，她的光彩
竟使我的敌人倾倒，致使他变本加厉
日复一日把我逼近令她心碎的角隅
我们都心碎了，啊，雾中的孩子
你怎么一点也没有想过悲惨的结局呢？
我不能给你留下什么；你会成为厚厚的书籍
你会叫我避讳某些词汇，呵，你，我雾中的亲人
死守在白玉中要看我怎样偃旗息鼓

5

还有你，纯洁的朗读，我病中的水果
我自己也是水果依偎你秋天的气味
醉心于影子和明净空气中的衣裳
你会念念不忘我这双手指，而他们
却酿成了新的胁迫，命运弦上最敏感的音节
瞧瞧我们怎样更换着：你与我，我与陌生的心
唉，一地之于另一地是多么虚幻

6

你又带了什么消息，我和谐的伴侣
急躁的性格，像今天傍晚的西风
一路风尘仆仆，只为一句忘却的话
贫困而又生动，是夜半星星的密谈者
是的，东西比我们富于耐心

rushing for a date due to the tears of others. I can't
change them no matter what; in the solitude of a clear mirror
their tenacity becomes the depths of my dreams

4

That, that apple of the naïve mother's eye: her splendor
sweeps away my enemy, aggravating him
cornering me shattering her corner day after day
Our hearts shattered, O child of fog
why didn't you think of a tragic end?
I can't leave behind anything for you; you become thick books
telling me to veto certain words. O you, my kin of fog
in white jade clinging to see how I give in

5

And your refined reading, fruits of my illness
I am the fruit snuggling up to your autumn scent
intoxicated by shadows and robes in the bright clear air
You'll keep thinking of my ten fingers, but they
have become a new threat, syllables most sensitive on fate's strings
Look how we are renewed: you and me, me and a foreign heart
Sigh, what an illusion, comparing one place to another

6

What news do you bring, my cordial companion
hot-tempered like this westerly evening wind
worn and weary from the road, all for a line of oblivion
Poor yet vivid, the confidant of midnight stars
Yes, things are richer in patience than we are

而我们比别人更富于果敢
在这个坚韧的世界上来来往往
你，连同你的书，都会磨成芬芳的尘埃

7

你是我最新的朋友（也许最后一个）
与我的父母踏着同一步伐成长
而你的脸，却反映出异样的风貌
我喜欢你等待我的样子，这天凉的季节
我们紧握的手也一天天变凉
你把我介绍成一扇温和的门，而进去后
却是你自己饰满陌生礼品的房间
我们同看一朵花瓣的时候，不知你怎么想

8

这夜晚风声加紧，你们来到我的心中
代替了我设想的动作，也代替了书桌前的我
让我变成了一个欲言不能的影子
日子会一天天变美，洁白无瑕，正像
我们心目中的任何一件小东西
活着？活着就是改掉缺点
就是走向英勇的高处，在落叶纷纷中
依然保持我们躯体的崇高和健全

richer than others in courage
To and fro in this world of fortitude
you and your books will be crushed into fragrant motes of dust

7

You are my newest friend (perhaps the last)
growing up in step with my parents
Yet your face conveys a different air
I like the way you wait for me, this cool season
Tightly clasped, our hands turn cold day after day
You introduce me as a gentle door, once entered
it turns out to be your room adorned with strange gifts
As we both look at a petal, what are your thoughts

8

Wind quickens tonight. You come to my heart
replacing my planned moves, then me before my writing desk
turning me into a wordless shadow
Life beautifies day after day, white and spotless, like
anything minute in our hearts
Live? To live is to improve
to walk to the height of valor, to maintain among
falling leaves the noble health of our bodies

深秋的故事

向深秋再走几日
我就会接受她震悚的背影
她开口说江南如一棵树
我眼前的景色便开始结果
开始迢递；呵，她所说的那种季候
仿佛正对着逆流而上的某个人
开花，并穿越信誓的拱桥

落下一片叶
就知道是甲子年
我身边的老人们
菊花般升腾，坠地
情人们的地方蚕食其他的地方
她便说江南如她的发型
没有雨天，纸片都叠成了乳燕

而我渐渐登上了晴朗的梯子
诗行中有栏杆，我眼前的地图

开始飘零，收敛
我用手指清理着落花
一遍又一遍地叨念自己的名字，仿佛

那有着许多小石桥的江南
我哪天会经过，正如同
经过她寂静的耳畔
她的袖口藏着皎美的气候
而整个那地方

Late Autumn Story

A few more days to late Autumn
I'll accept her trembling silhouette
She declares, *Jiangnan is like a tree*
and the scene before my eyes bears fruit
and recedes; ah, the season she describes
appears to blossom before someone traveling
upstream, through the arched bridge of a vow

A leaf falls
You know it is the first year of the zodiac
Like chrysanthemums, old folks
rise around me, born anew
Sites of lovers nibbling at other sites
So she says Jiangnan is like her hairstyle
Without rainy days, pieces of paper are folded into young swallows

I gradually mount the sunny ladder
Rails exist in verses, the map before my eyes

starts to float and fall, converging
I use my fingers to clear away the fallen flowers
mumbling my name again and again, as if

Jiangnan were there with its many stone bridges
Someday I'll pass by, like
passing by her quiet ears
Her cuffs hide a splendid weather
and that entire place

也会在她的脸上张望
也许我们不会惊动那些老人们
他们菊花般升腾坠地
清晰并且芬芳

will look around on her face
Perhaps we won't startle the old folks
Like chrysanthemums they rise and fall
clear and fragrant

灯芯绒幸福的舞蹈

1

“它是光”，我抬起头，驰心
向外，“她理应修饰。”
我的目光注视舞台，
它由各种器皿搭就构成。
我看见的她，全是为我
而舞蹈，我没有在意

她大部分真实。台上
锣鼓喧天，人群熙攘；
她的影儿守舍身后，
不像她的面目，衬着灯芯绒
我直看她姣美的式样，待到
天凉，第一声叶落，我对

近身的人士说；“秀色可餐。”
我跪下身，不顾尘垢，
而她更是四肢生辉。出场
入场，声色更迭；变幻的器皿
模棱两可；各种用途之间
她的灯芯绒磨损，陈旧。

天地悠悠，我的五官狂蹦
乱跳，而舞台，随造随拆。
衣着乃变幻：“许多夕照后
东西会越变越美。”
我站起，面无愧色，可惜
话声未落，就听得一声叹喟。

The Blissful Corduroy Dance

1

It is light. I lift my head, heart longing
outward. *She should dress up.*
My gaze fixed on the stage
built by all kinds of vessels.
The she I see is there
to dance for me. I don't mind

that she is *mostly* authentic. Onstage
deafening gongs and drums, crowds;
her shadow guarding from behind,
unlike her looks, against corduroy
I stare at her gorgeous motifs until it turns
chilly. At the sound of a fallen leaf, I

say to those nearby, *What a feast for the eyes.*
I kneel, not caring for dirt and dust, as she turns
even more sparklingly alive. Enter the dancer,
the audience, voices alternating; vessels transform
ambiguously; in between each function
her corduroy is worn-out, outmoded.

Drifting world, my five senses leap
madly. The stage is set up and torn down.
Clothes metamorphose. *After myriad
sunsets, things become lovelier.*
I stand up, unembarrassed. Alas,
before a word is spoken, I hear a sigh.

2

我看到自己软弱而且美，
我舞蹈，旋转中不动。
他的梦，梦见了梦，明月皎皎，
映出灯芯绒——我的格式
又是世界的格式；
我和他合一舞蹈。

我并非含混不清，
只因生活是件真事情。
“君子不器，”我严格，
却一贯忘怀自己，
我是酒中的光，
是分币的企图，如此妩媚。

我更不想以假乱真；
只因技艺纯熟（天生的）
我之于他才如此陌生。
我的衣裳丝毫未改，
我的影子也热泪盈盈，
这一点，我和他理解不同。

我最终要去责怪他。
可他，不会明白这番道理，
除非他再来一次，设身处地，
他才不会那样挑选我
像挑选一只鲜果。
“唉，遗失的只与遗失者在一起。”
我只好长长叹息。

1986

2

I see my weakness and beauty.
I dance, I keep still while whirling.
His dream, a dreamed dream, a bright moon,
mirroring corduroy—my style
the world's style;
I dance with him.

Not that I am obscure,
life is something real.
An educated man is not a pot. I am strict,
yet always forgetting myself.
I am the light within wine
a currency's ambition, so charming.

But I won't mix the fake with the real;
only through virtuosic skills (a natural talent)
I feel so foreign to him.
My skirt unchanged,
my shadow suffused with tears.
On this issue, we do not agree.

I'll scold him sooner or later.
But he does not understand this;
unless he comes again, puts himself in my shoes,
he wouldn't pick me the way
he picks a fresh apple.
Sigh, a loss only stays with the one who loses something.
I can only heave a long sigh.

1986

楚王梦雨

我要衔接过去一个人的梦，
纷纷雨滴同享的一朵闲云；
我的心儿要跳得同样迷乱，
宫殿春叶般生，酒沫鱼样跃，
让那个对饮的，也举落我的手。
我的手扪脉，空亭吐纳云雾，
我的梦正梦见另一个梦呢。

枯木上的灵芝，水腰系上绢帛，
西边的飞蛾探听夕照的虚实。
它们刚辞别幽所，必定见过
那个一直轻呼我名字的人，
那个可能鸣翔．也可能开落，
给人佩玉，又叫人狐疑的空址。
她的践约可能是澌澌潮湿的。

真奇怪，雨滴还未发落的前夕，
我已感到了周身潮湿呢：
青翠的竹子可以拧出水，
山谷来的风吹入它们的内心，
而我的耳朵似乎飞到了半空，
或者是凝伫而燃烧吧，燃烧那个
一直戏睡在里面．那湫隘的人。

还燃烧她的耳朵，烧成灰烟，
决不叫她偷听我心的饥饿。
你看，这醉我的世界含满了酒，
竹子也含了晨曦和岁月。
它们萧萧的声音多痛，多痛，

The Prince of Chu Dreams of Rain

I want to connect to the dream of someone from the past—
an idle cloud shared by endless raindrops.
My heart wants to leap into bewilderment,
a palace appears like spring leaves, frothing wine leaps like fish.
Let the one who drinks opposite me lift and drop my hand.
My hand pulses, an empty pavilion exhales clouds and mist.
My dream is dreaming another dream.

Reishi mushrooms on a withered tree, silk around its waist.
Moths from the west probe the sunset;
barely away from their love nest, they must have seen
the one whispering my name.
The address of no one might thunder and soar, open and fall,
bestowing jade, raising doubts.
She might keep her appointment, dripping wet.

How odd, on the eve of raindrops
my body already feels wet:
water wrung from crisp green bamboo shoots,
wind from the canyon blows into their hearts.
Yet my ears seem to fly into midair,
or stand and burn, burning the petty
woman who feigns sleep inside them.

And burning her ears into ashes,
so she can never eavesdrop into my starving heart.
Look, this self-indulgent world is full of wine.
Even bamboos are tinged with dawns and years.
How painful their bleak voices, how painful.

愈痛我愈要剥它，剥成七孔，
那么我的病也是世界的痛。

请你不要再聆听我了，莫名的人。
我知道你在某处，隔风嬉戏。
空白的梦中之梦，假的荷叶，
令我彻反难眠的住址。
如果雨滴有你，火焰岂不是我？
人神道殊，而殊途同归，
我要，我要，爱上你神的热泪。

1987. 6. 12 威茨堡大学

The more pain the more I yearn to peel them into seven holes.
My pain is also the world's pain.

Nameless one, please don't listen to me.
I know you are somewhere playing in the wind.
A blank dream of a dream, a fake lotus leaf,
the address leading me to insomnia.
Am I not the flame if you live in each drop of rain?
Gods and men on different paths reach the same end.
I want, I want to love your godly, hot tears.

June 12, 1987—University of Würzburg

早春二月

太阳曾经照亮我；在重庆，一颗
露珠的心清早含着图像朵朵
我绕过一片又一片空气；铁道
让列车疼得逃光，留杜鹃轻歌
我说，顶峰你好，还有梧桐松柏
无论上下，请让我幽会般爱着
在湖南，阳光照亮童年的眼睛
我的手长大，抚摸的道路变短
尘埃绕城市袅袅地跳循环舞
喇叭像弟弟，车轮就是万花筒
换牙的疼变成屁股上的伤疤
果实把我捉到树上，狠狠把我
摔落。哎，我感到我今天还活着
活在一个纸做的假地方；春天
咕咕叫，太阳像庸医到处摸摸
摸摸这个提前或是推迟了的
时代，摸摸这个世界的乌托邦
哎，潜龙勿用，好比一根烂绳索。

1988.3.18 特里雅大学

Early Spring, February

The sun once shone on me; in Chongqing, a drop
of dew with clarity, images enfolding in petals
I go around the air, patch by patch; railways
harm trains until they flee, sparing a light cuckoo's song
I say, *Hello summit, wutong trees, pines and cypresses*
High or low, please let me love like in a secret rendezvous
In Hunan, sunlight kindles childhood eyes
My hands grow, the path they fondle is cut short
Dust swirls around the city and dances round and round
Like a brother the trumpet wheels a kaleidoscope
Teething pain turns into a scar on the buttocks
A fruit grabs me up a tree and harshly
drops me. Why, I still feel alive today
in a pseudo place made of paper; spring
coos, the sun touches everywhere like a quack
touching this early or belated
era, touching this world's utopia
Ah, a hidden dragon waits for action, as futile as rotten rope

March 18, 1988—Trier University

死亡的比喻

死亡猜你的年纪
认为你这时还年轻
它站立的角度的尽头
恰好是孩子的背影
繁花，感冒和黄昏
死亡说时间还充裕

多么温顺的小手
问你要一件东西
你给它像给了个午睡
凉荫里游着闲鱼

死亡猜你的年纪
你猜猜孩子的人品
孩子猜孩子的蜜橘

吃了的东西，长身体
没吃的东西，添运气
孩子对孩子坐着
死亡对孩子躺着
孩子对你站起

死亡猜你的年纪
认为你这时还年轻
孩子猜你的背影
睁着好吃的眼睛

1987. 1. 14 Königstein

Death Metaphor

death can guess your age
think you are still young
the end of its straight angle
children's silhouettes by chance
flourishing flowers, cold and dusk
death says there's plenty of time

such a docile hand
asks you for something
you give it like it's a nap
fish swim at ease in the shade

death can guess your age
guess the children's character
children guess children's tangerines

things eaten help the body grow
things uneaten bring more luck
children sit before children
death lies down before them
who stand up to you

death can guess your age
think you are still young
children guess your silhouette
it fights for tasty eyes

January 14, 1987—Königstein

麓山的回忆

你在山的下面起舞
不再跟其它的手臂牵连
天欲落叶，树欲啼鸟
阳光普照你的胸前
空气新鲜，你不怕
你的另一半会交付谁
谁是黑暗，水果的里面
谁是灯，开启之前
谁去山顶的上面
书未读完，自己入眠？

1987. 3. 7 Königstein

Memory of Mount Lu

you dance below the mountain
no longer tangled in other arms
leaves falling from the sky, birds chirping from trees
sunlight illumines your chest
you don't fear fresh air
who your other half will hand over
who is darkness   inside a fruit
who is a lamp   before switching it on
who goes up the summit
books unfinished, asleep?

March 7, 1987—Königstein

云天

在我最孤独的时候
我总是凝望云天
我不知道我是在祈祷
或者，我已经幸存?

总是有个细小的声音
在我内心的迷宫嘤嘤
它将引我到更远
虽然我多么不情愿

到黄昏，街坊和向日葵
都显得无比宁静
我在想，那只密林深处
练习闪烁的小鹿

是否已被那只沉潜的猛虎
吃掉，当春叶繁衍?
唉，莫名发疼的细小声音
我祈祷着同样的牺牲……

我想我的好运气
终有一天会来临
我将被我终生想象着的
寥若星辰的
那么几个佼佼者
阅读，并且喜爱。

1988. 1. 18

Cloud Sky

in my loneliest moments
I gaze at the cloud sky
I don't know if I'm praying
or survived

always a tiny voice
in my heart's labyrinth
leading me to a farther place
despite my reluctance

at dusk, the neighborhood and sunflowers
are an unparalleled quiet
I wonder, deep in the forest
has the fawn practicing its glow

been devoured by a submerged
tiger, multiplying as spring leaves?
sigh, the tiny voice aches for no reason
I pray for the same sacrifice . . .

I reckon my luck
will come one day
I'll be read, adored
by the few and rare
outstanding figures
I've pictured all my life

January 18, 1988

苍蝇

我越看你越像一个人
清秀的五官，纹丝不动
我想深入你嵯峨的内心
五脏俱全，随你的血液
沿周身晕眩，并以微妙的肝胆
扩大月亮的盈缺

我绕着你踱了很多圈
哦，苍蝇，我对你满怀憧憬

你的天地就是我的天地
你的春秋叫我忘记花叶
如此我迁入你的寿命和积习
与你浑然一体，歌舞营营
听梦中的情侣唏嘘

你看，不，我看，黄昏来了
这场失火的黄昏
灾难的气味多难闻
让我们不再跟世界一起紊乱

哦，苍蝇，小小的伤痛
小小的随便的死亡
好像你蹉跎舌上的
另一番滋味，另一种美馔

Fly

The more I see you the more human you seem
Five delicate senses, motionless
I want to penetrate your rugged mind
vital organs intact, in your blood
I spin with the whole body, expanding moonlight
with subtle courage

I pace around you in circles
O fly, I long for you

Your universe is mine
Your years make me forget flowers and leaves
So I move into your life and habits
merge with you, singing, dancing
listening to lovers sigh or sob in dreams

Look, no, let me look, dusk is here
It catches fire
How the smell of disaster reeks
Let's not join that chaotic world

O fly, a small wound
a small casual death
like another taste, another delicacy
wasting on your tongue

在夜莺婉转的英格兰
一个德国间谍的爱与死（组诗）

Was it a vision, or a waking dream?
Fled is that music:—Do I wake or sleep?
—J. Keats

1

没有奶油。战争啃着发绿霉的面包皮。
潜艇在这个“心”形的港湾吐出了子夜
和我。我把我自己黑箭一般射了出去。

为了日耳曼的最后一击，我咽下心跳。
一只温顺的野山羊有一会儿拦住我的
去路。暗中的每件小事物都像手牵着手。

夜莺婉转。我分辨不清是真还是假。
一股暖流蓦然涌上心头，当我看见
远处窗口她的白色侧影。灯闪了三下。

珍贵的抵达！“不知为了什么，我的心
是这般忧伤，”——我的暗语；“一个古老的
传说，我总是不能遗忘”——她的回答。

Love and Death of a German Spy in the England of a Sweet Nightingale

[a lyric sequence]

Was it a vision, or a waking dream?
Fled is that music:—Do I wake or sleep?
—John Keats

1

No butter. War chews on moldy crusts of bread.
In a heart-shaped harbor, submarines exhale midnight
and me. I fling myself out like a black arrow.

For the last German shot, I swallow my heartbeat.
A gentle wild goat temporarily blocks my
way. In the dark, all small things go hand in hand.

Sweet nightingale. I can't tell the real from the fake.
A sudden rush of warmth pours into my heart when I see
her white silhouette by a distant window. Lights flicker thrice.

Precious arrival! *My heart is so inexplicably*
sad—my argot; *An ancient*
legend I can never forget—her response.

2

夜莺婉转。济慈的夜莺隐入黎明。
黎明在换哨。将是一个万里无云的天晴。
他们将某种几何图案变了又变——

人的一贯伎俩。从小阁楼的窗口，水上
蓝色的现实涌进我焦灼的望远镜
像我内心鲜活的纷纭变幻。但那唯一的

不会变。“变”其实摆脱不了“不变”的
愿望。于是什么也没变。于是四十只
军舰。历史正悄悄打开新的一页。

她把拭汗的毛巾递给我。还有咖啡。
芳香的奶油揩在整齐的面包片上。我们
歇一会儿。窗下一个醉汉走过，歌唱着

2

Sweet nightingale. Keats's nightingale looms at dawn.
Dawn on guard mount. Soon a vast sky.
Changing a geometric pattern again and again—

Man's usual tricks. From an attic window, on water
blue reality pours itself into my anxious binoculars
as vivid as myriad changes in my heart. But that one and only

stays unchanged. *Change* can't break away from *unchanging*
hope. So nothing has changed. So forty
warships. History is quietly turning the page.

She passes me a towel for the sweat. And coffee.
Sweet butter is spread on neatly sliced bread. We
rest awhile. Under the window a drunkard walks past, singing

3

我问："你是谁……也就是说，你怎么
是现在的你？"她甩了甩长辫，说：
"喏，你瞧，我正代替另一个人活着。"

"我们在半道上截住了她，那可怜的
小学教员，一个无辜的人——跟我一样，
然后就是那一套张冠李戴的把戏。"

"那么你俩长得一样？""五官倒是
差不多，只是我或许漂亮一点儿……"
她闭上眼睛回忆一年前的那一幕

像回忆她的妹妹，她的手撕着
桌几上的落花。"那么你呢？"她问，
"我嘛，很简单，不过得过几枚勋章。"我说。

3

I ask, *Who are you?* Meaning, *How could you*
be the current you? She swings her long braid and says,
Look, I'm living for someone else.

We stopped her midway, the poor
elementary teacher, an innocent soul—just like me,
followed by those confusing tricks.

So you both look alike? Quite so
our faces, but I'm probably prettier . . .
She closes her eyes to recall a scene from last year

as if recalling her sister. She tears up
flowers fallen on the table. *And you?* she asks.
I reply, *I've received some medals. That's all.*

4

他歌唱着，歌唱着的醉汉打窗下
走过。中午的阳光晒烫了教堂的尖端。
没有孩子在揭开大海干涩的皮肤。

奶油在消融，腥味的风梳过松柏林，
吹动檐角的晒衣索。她去井边汲水，
把凉水洒向汗晶晶的发额和颈脖。

醉汉走过，歌唱着；无垠的天空
铺织着瓦，在蝉儿的聒噪里变得
更蓝。蓝得像她的美目。我心跳。

我们的嘴唇粘在一起。远处，军舰
仍变着队形操练。醉汉走过，
歌唱着。我们突然领悟了什么。

4

He sings, the singing drunkard walks past
the window. The afternoon sun scalds the church's peak.
No child to unveil the dry seaskin.

The butter is melting, a reeking wind combs cypress-pines,
blowing clotheslines along the eaves. She draws water from a well,
sprinkles it over her sweaty hair, forehead, and neck.

The drunkard walks past, singing; a vast sky
lays tiles. In the clamor of cicadas, it turns
bluer. As blue as her *beaux yeux*. My heartbeat.

Our lips are glued. Afar warships are yet
in their battle array. The drunkard walks past,
singing. We suddenly realize something.

5

星期三在换哨。醉汉从窗下走过
歌唱着。“主啊。是时候了！”
换哨的脸无聊地重复着。主啊，你看看

我们的新玩意：小巧的步话机
像你的夜莺：哦，BEHEMOTH，小宝贝
看你今儿怎样呼风唤雨。主啊。

变红的白云，危险的白云，主啊
调遣你的王牌军。夜莺婉转。
伦敦硝烟一片，值夜班的艾略特在研究

火。水赶来急救。可这儿，可这儿
仍是沉寂，除了夜莺。主啊调遣
你可怕的鸽子。潜艇的美人鱼，阿门！

5

Guards shifting on Wednesday. Under the window the drunkard
walks past,
singing. *O Lord, it's time!*
Bored faces repeat themselves. O Lord, look

at our new toy: a cute walkie-talkie
like your nightingale: Oh, Behemoth, darling,
let's see how you summon the wind and rain. O Lord.

Blushing white clouds, dangerous white clouds, O Lord,
dispatch your elite troops. Sweet nightingale.
London in smoke, T.S. Eliot is studying fire

on the night shift. Water rushes to its rescue. But here, here
a stillness save for a nightingale. O Lord, dispatch
your terrible doves. Submarine mermaids, amen!

6

夜莺婉转。我们闭目等待。
我们在最黑暗的夜里祈祷。
我们等待火光冲天，照亮海洋与

玫瑰。我和我最心爱的人在一起
等待，玫瑰就是等待。
那醉汉的歌声在海边徘徊。

后来他们开火了。（醉汉走向窗口）
但我不知道是谁对谁
开火。一切开火都是射向不痛的虚幻？

而我痛。我最后的瞳孔留着
她的微笑。甜美的微笑，请留一留！
我似乎听见她扑向谁的怀抱。

谁战胜了谁？我永久的疑惑……

　　　　……我将永远没有奶油。

1989 特里尔

6

Sweet nightingale. We close our eyes and wait.
We pray in the darkest night.
We wait for flames to spring up high, illumining the sea and

roses. Together I wait with my most
beloved, roses mean waiting.
The drunkard's singing loiters by the sea.

Later, they open fire. (The drunkard walks to the window.)
But I don't know who is firing
at whom. Is everything firing at a painless illusion?

I am hurting. Her smile remains in my last
pupil. Sweet smile, please stay!
I can almost hear her run into someone's arms.

Who has beaten whom? My eternal puzzle . . .

. . . I will never have butter.

1989, Trier

德国士兵雪曼斯基的死刑

　　俄语是我的命运。
国境上，我这孤儿
在面包与风车的边缘长大。
啊，如画的村庄。
除了母舌德语，我的俄语
也长得飞快，
快得超过秘密的列车我的牙齿我的年龄
和树。
Kakayaharoshayapogoda!
嘿，多美的天气！
　　后来战争爆发了
我先是失去了充满白昼和石头的
希腊；尤加利树和泉水淙淙的
音乐，令我沉默。
三个月我没说一句话，
对长官也从不说 jawohl
后来他们调遣我去俄国：
火的聂瓦河，
破烂的斯大林格勒，
这一切都像是我一个人的过错。
真的，语言就是世界，而世界
并不用语言来宽恕。
哎，恨的岁月，褴褛的语言，
我还要忍受你多久？
　　后来我们驻扎
某个村庄，虽然是第一次来
对我却像来过多次。什么，déjà vu？
“我们最熟悉的反而是
陌生的地方，对吗，上尉？”

Schermanski the German Soldier's Death Sentence

Russian is my destiny.
An orphan on the frontier,
I grew up on the border of bread and windmills.
O village, like a painting.
Like my mother tongue German, my Russian
flew like lightning,
faster than the secret train my teeth my age
and trees.
Kakaya sevodnya khoroshaya pogoda!
Such wonderful weather!
Later, war broke out.
First I lost a Greece full of daylight
and rocks; eucalyptus and music of a running
stream silenced me.
For three months, I said nothing,
not even a *Jawohl* to the officers.
Later they transferred me to Russia:
the Neva in flames,
Stalingrad in tatters,
everything seemed like my fault.
Truly, language is the world, and the world
needs no language to forgive.
Ah, years of hatred, shabby language,
how long must I put up with you?
Later we were stationed
at a village. It was my first time there,
yet it seemed as if I'd visited it countless times. What, déjà vu?
What strikes us as most familiar
is the foreign, isn't it, Captain?

上尉说：“雪曼斯基，
我们得修一座暗堡
像尖刀插在敌人的心脏！”
因为俄国话，
我被派去搞鸡蛋、鲜奶及其它给养。
于是，我每天出入街坊和篱墙，
十月的阳光照彻我流水般的影子，
我欢快得像舒伯特的“鳟鱼”。
我用灵活的舌头弹开门帘
装作布谷鸟远逗绯红的卡佳
——卡佳，你准备好了吗？
　　今天给我十个红苹果。
卡佳的腋下有点狐臭，跟我一样
但不要紧；通夜，明月
热乎乎地在我们身上嬉戏。
我们第一次的身体
不是像两个词汇，碰了，变成成语？
卡佳，Ya tebya liubliu!
——告诉我，这句德语该怎么说？
我答道，Ich liebe dich, 卡佳！
　　后来我们的暗堡废了，
游击队，嘿，美丽的卡佳。
　　军事法庭判我叛国罪。
给我四十八小时的时间。
我用二十四小时潜逃，
被揪回；又用十四小时求恩赦，
我写到：Bitte, bitte, Gnade!
被驳回；他们再给我十个小时
八个小时，六个小时，五个小时；
后来战地牧师来了，
慈祥得像永恒：
可永恒替代不了我。
正如一颗子弹替代不了我，

The Captain replied, *Schermanski,*
we must build a bunker
like stabbing a knife in the enemy's heart!
Because of my Russian,
I was sent to hunt for eggs, fresh milk, and other food.
So every day I went in and out of the quarter through wattles,
the October sun shining through my shadow like flowing water.
I rejoiced like Schubert's "Trout."
I flicked open door curtains with a lively tongue
in the disguise of a cuckoo, teased the blushing Katya
—*Katya, are you ready?*
  Give me ten red apples.
Katya's armpits, like mine, smelled
but that was alright; all night long a bright moon
frolics warmly on our bodies.
Our bodies, for the first time—
weren't they like two vocabularies turning into idioms when they collide?
Katya, *Ya tebya lyublyu!*
—*Tell me, how do you pronounce this German phrase?*
I replied, *Ich liebe dich, Katya!*
          Later we deserted our bunker,
guerillas, hey, pretty Katya.
          I was court-martialed for treason.
I was given forty-eight hours.
I used twenty-four hours to flee
but was recaptured; another fourteen to beg for mercy.
I wrote *Bitte, bitte, Gnade!*
but was rejected; they gave me another ten hours,
eight hours, six hours, five hours;
here came the army chaplain,
kind as eternity:
but an eternity like a bullet
could not replace me.

我，雪曼斯基，好一个人！
牧师哭了，搂紧我，亲吻我：
——孩子，孩子，Du bist nicht verloren!
　　还有一点儿时间，你要不要写封信？
　　你念，我写——可您会俄语吗？
　　上帝会各种语言，我的孩子。
于是，我急迫地说，卡佳，我的蜜拉娅，
蜜拉娅，卡佳，我还有十分钟，
黎明还有十分钟，
秋天还有五分钟，
我们还有两分钟，
一分钟，半分钟，
　　十秒，八秒，五秒，
　　二秒：Lebewohl! 卡佳，蜜拉娅！

　　嘿，请射我的器官。
别射我的心。
卡佳，我的蜜拉娅……
我死掉了死——真的，死是什么？
死就像别的人死了一样。

I, Schermanski, what a man!
The chaplain cried, then held and kissed me:
—*My child, my child,* du bist nicht verloren!
  We still have some time, would you like to write a letter?
  Just say, I'll write—but sir, do you know Russian?
  God knows all languages, my child.
So I said in haste, *Katya, my sweet,*
dear Katya, I've only ten more minutes,
ten more minutes for daybreak,
five more minutes for autumn,
we have two more minutes,
one minute, half a minute,
    ten seconds, eight seconds, five seconds,
    two seconds: Lebewohl! *Katya my sweet!*

    Shoot me in the organs.
Not my heart.
Katya, my sweet . . .
I die a death—indeed, what is death?
Death is to die like others.

椅子坐进冬天……

椅子坐进冬天，一共
有三张，寒冷是肌肉，
它们一字儿排开，
害怕逻辑，天使中，
没有三个谁会
坐在它们身上，等着
滑过冰河的理发师，虽然
前方仍是一个大镜子，
喜鹊收拾着小分币。

风的织布机，织着四周。
主人，是一个虚无，远远
站在郊外，呵着热气，
浓眉大眼地数着椅子：
不用碰它即可拿掉
那个中间，
如果把左边的那张
移植到最右边，不停地——

如此刺客，在宇宙的
心间。突然
三张椅子中那莫须有的
第四张，那唯一的，
也坐进了冬天。像那年冬天……
　　　　　　　　……我爱你。

1995

Chairs Sit Their Way into Winter . . .

Chairs sit their way into winter: three
in all, the cold their flesh,
spread in a row.
They fear logic. Among angels
no trio will sit
on them to wait for the barber
to skate across an iced-over river, though
ahead lies a large mirror
with magpies collecting coins.

The wind's loom weaves the surroundings.
Owned by a void in the distance,
standing on the outskirts, exhaling hot air,
counting chairs with thick eyebrows, eyes wide:
take away the middle chair
without touching it.
If the one on the left
always shifts to the far right—

such an assassin at the heart
of the universe. Suddenly
among three chairs, a phantom
fourth, the one and only
also sits its way into winter. Like that winter . . .
. . . I love you.

1995

卡夫卡致菲丽丝（十四行组诗）

Heute ist wieder nichts, Liebste, traurig.
—Kafka

1

我叫卡夫卡，如果您记得
我们是在M.B.家相遇的。
当您正在灯下浏览相册，
一股异香袭进了我心底。

我奇怪的肺朝向您的手，
像孔雀开屏，乞求着赞美。
您的影在钢琴架上颤抖，
朝向您的夜，我奇怪的肺。

像圣人一刻都离不开神，
我时刻惦着我的孔雀肺。
我替它打开血腥的笼子，

去啊，我说，去贴紧那颗心：
“我可否将您比作红玫瑰？”
屋里浮满枝叶，屏息注视。

Kafka to Felice [a sequence of sonnets]

Nothing again today, dearest, sad.
—Kafka

1

I am Kafka, you might recall
we met at M.B.'s house. When you were
browsing the picture album under a lamp,
an exotic scent invaded my heart.

My strange lungs face your hands,
like a peacock flaunting its feathers, pleading
for praise. Your shadow trembles on the piano,
my strange lungs facing your night.

Like a saint who never leaves God,
I keep thinking of my peacock lungs.
I open a bloody cage for them.

Go, I say, cling to the heart: *May I compare*
you to a red rose? Leaves and branches float
in the house, gazing with bated breath.

2

布拉格的雪夜，从交叉的小巷
跑过小偷地下党以及失眠者。
大地竖起耳朵，风中杨柳转向，
火在萧瑟？不，那可是神的使者。

他们坚持说来的是一位天使，
灰色的雨衣，冻得淌着鼻血
他们说他不是那么可怕，伫止
在电话亭旁，斜视满天的电线，

伤心的样子，人们都想走近他，
摸他。但是，谁这样想，谁就失去
了他。剧烈的狗吠打开了灌木。

一条路闪光。他的背影真高大。
我听见他打开地下室的酒橱，
我真想哭。我的双手冻得麻木。

2

On a snowy night in Prague, through scissoring lanes,
thieves, the underground and the insomniac run.
The earth pricks up its ears, willows veer in the wind,
is it the rustle of fire? No, that is God's messenger.

They insist that an angel has come: in a
gray raincoat, frozen until his nose bleeds.
They say he isn't that frightening, that he stops by
a phone booth, leering at the sky of wires,

looking sad. They wish to approach him, to
touch him. Yet whoever thinks of doing so
will lose him. A violent dog barks open the bushes.

A road glitters. His towering silhouette.
I hear him open the basement cellaret. How I long
for tears. My hands have gone numb with the cold.

3

致命的仍是突围。那最高的是
鸟。在下面就意味着仰起头颅。
哦，鸟！我们刚刚呼出你的名字，
你早成了别的，歌曲融满道路，

像孩子嘴中的糖块化成未来
的某一天。哦，怎样的一天，出了
多少事。我看见一辆列车驶来
载着你的形象。菲丽丝，我的鸟

我永远接不到你，鲜花已枯焦
因为我们迎接的永远是虚幻——
上午背影在前，下午它又倒挂

身后。然而，什么是虚幻？我祈祷。
小雨点硬着头皮将事物敲响：
我们的突围便是无尽的转化。

3

Yet fatal is the breakthrough. Highest
is a bird. To stay below signifies skulls looking up.
O bird! Just as we breathe out your name,
you've turned into something else, songs flood the road,

like a lump of sugar in a child's mouth, melting
into a day from the future. What a day, so
much has happened. I see a train
carrying your image. Felice, my bird,

I can never catch you. Flowers have withered
because what we greet is always the illusion—
the silhouette moves ahead in the morning, hangs upside

down from behind in the afternoon. But what is illusion? I pray.
Little raindrops brace themselves for striking at things aloud:
our breakthrough an infinite metamorphosis.

4

夜啊，你总是还够不上夜，
孤独，你总是还不够孤独！
地下室里我谛听阴郁的

橡树（它将雷电吮得破碎）
而我，总是难将自己够着，
时间啊，哪儿会有足够的

梅花鹿，一边跑一边更多——
仿佛那消耗的只是风月
办公楼的左边，布谷鸟说：
活着，无非是缓慢的失血。

我真愿什么会把我载走，
载到一个没有我的地方；
那些打字机，唱片和星球，
都在魔鬼的舌头下旋翻。

4

O night, you are always less than night,
solitude, always less than solitude!
From the basement I listen to a gloomy

oak (it sucks thunder and lightning into pieces)
while I am always less than myself.
O time, where can we find enough

sika deer, increasing as they run—
as if to spend wind and moon.
On the left of an office building, a cuckoo says,
To live is simply to lose slow blood.

How I wish something could carry me away,
to somewhere without me;
typewriters, records, and planets
twist and turn under Satan's tongue.

5

什么时候人们最清晰地看见
自己？是月夜，石头心中的月夜。
凡是活动的，都从分裂的岁月

走向幽会。哦，一切全都是镜子！
我写作。蜘蛛嗅嗅月亮的腥味。
文字醒来，拎着裙裾，朝向彼此，

并在地板上忧心忡忡地起舞。
真不知它们是上帝的儿女，或
从属于魔鬼的势力。我真想哭。
有什么突然摔碎，它们便隐去

隐回事物里，现在只留下阴影
对峙着那些仍然朗响的沉寂。
菲丽丝，今天又没有你的来信。
孤独中我沉吟着奇妙的自己。

5

When do men see themselves most
clearly? Moonlit night in a stone's heart.
All that moves will walk from shattered years

to a rendezvous. O, all is a mirror!
I write. A spider sniffs the reeking moon.
Words wake up, lift their skirts, face each other,

and waltz away on the floor with heavy hearts.
Who knows if they are God's children
or belong to Satan. I want to cry.
Suddenly something smashes. They hide

back into things, shadows left behind
to face the resonant stillness.
Felice, again there is no letter from you.
In solitude I mutter to my intriguing self.

6

阅读就是谋杀；我不喜欢
孤独的人读我，那灼急的
呼吸令我生厌；他们揪起
书，就像揪起自己的器官。

这滚烫的夜呵，遍地苦痛。
他们用我呵斥勃起的花，
叫神鸡零狗碎无言以答，
叫面目可憎者无地自容，

自己却溜达在妓院药店，
跟不男不女的人们周旋，
讽刺一番暴君，谈谈凶年；

天上的星星高喊："烧掉我！"
布拉格的水喊："给我智者。"
墓碑沉默：读我就是杀我。

6

Reading is murder; I don't like
being read by lonely men, their urgent
breathing disgusts me; they grab
books like grabbing their own organs.

O scalding night, misery everywhere.
They use me to berate flowers that sprout,
to render God fragmented and speechless
and repulsive men too ashamed to appear,

while they linger around brothels and drugstores,
mingle with neither men nor women,
lampoon tyrants, discuss a lean year.

Stars yell, *Burn me!*
Water from Prague yells, *Send me a wise man.*
Quiet tombs: read me to kill me.

7

突然的散步：那驱策着我的血，
比夜更暗一点：血，戴上夜礼帽，
披上发腥的外衣，朝向那外面，
那些遨游的小生物。灯像恶枭；

别怕，这是夜，陌生的事物进入
我们，铸造我们。枯蛾紧揪着光，
作最后的祷告。生死突然交触，
我听见蛾们迷醉的舌头品尝

某个无限的开阔。突然的散步，
它们轻呼："向这边，向这边，不左
不右，非前非后，而是这边，怕不？"

只要不怕，你就是天使。快松开
自己，扔在路旁，更纯粹地向前。
别怕，这是风。铭记这浩大天籁。

7

A sudden stroll: blood spurs me on,
darker than night: blood dons a gentleman's hat of night,
puts on a musty coat, facing outward
to creatures that roam. Lamps resemble evil owls;

don't be afraid, this is night, foreign things enter
us, forge us. Withered moths clinch onto light
in their final prayer. Life and death in a sudden blend,
I hear bewitching moth tongues savor

the open space of infinity. A sudden stroll,
they whisper, *Here, here, neither left*
nor right, not front or back, right here, aren't you afraid?

Without fear, you will become an angel. Quick, loosen
yourself, throw yourself on the street and advance more purely.
Don't be afraid, this is wind. Remember the majesty of heavenly music.

8

很快就是秋天，而很快我就要
用另一种语言做梦；打开手掌，
打开树的盒子，打开锯屑之腰，

世界突然显现。这是她的落叶，
像棋子，被那棋手的胸怀照亮。
它们等在桥头路畔，时而挪前
一点，时而退缩，时而旋翻，总将

自己排成图案。可别乱碰它们，
它们的生存永远在家中度过；
采煤碴的孩子从霜结的房门
走出，望着光亮，脸上一片困惑。

列车载着温暖在大地上颤抖，
孩子被甩出车尾，和他的木桶，
像迸脱出图案。人类没有棋手……

8

Autumn soon and I will soon
dream in another language; palms open,
open tree boxes, opening the waist of sawdust,

the world suddenly emerges. Her fallen leaves,
like chess pieces lit up by the player's bosom.
They wait by the bridgehead. Now and then they shift
forward a little, recoil, flip, always arranging themselves

into a pattern. But don't mess with them,
their lives are spent at home;
a child who picks coal walks out of the frosty
door, gazing at light, baffled.

Trains loaded with warmth tremble over the earth,
the child and his bucket are thrown from the train's tail,
like a pattern bursting forth. There are no chess players among men . . .

9

人长久地注视它，那么，它
是什么？它是神，那么，神
是否就是它？若它就是神，
那么神便远远还不是它；

像光明稀释于光的本身，
那个它，以神的身份显现，
已经太薄弱，太苦，太局限。
它是神：怎样的一个过程！

世界显现于一棵菩提树，
而只有树本身知道自己
来得太远，太深，太特殊；

从翠密的叶间望见古堡，
我们这些必死的，矛盾的
测量员，最好是远远逃掉。

9

Men gaze at it for a long time, so what
is it? It is God, so is God
it? Were it God,
God would still be far from it;

like light diluted by light itself,
this *it* appears as God, already
too frail, too bitter, too reticent.
It is God: what a process!

The world appears as a Bodhi tree,
but only the tree itself knows
it is too far, too deep, too rarified;

gazing at the old castle through lush, dense leaves,
best that we the mortal, contradictory
surveyors flee far away.

伞

多少词

多少词，将与我终身绝缘
多少影子我不能骑进冬天
我这辈子大概不会落草为寇
但难说。那天我到峰顶吹冷风
其实是想踮足摸摸风筝跳荡的心
我孤绝。有一次跟自己对弈
不一会儿我就疯了。我愿是
潜艇里闲置得憋气的望远镜
别人死后我宁可做那个摆渡人
在某处，最深最深，山川如故
那该是几维空间，该有怎样的
炊烟袅娜于我的眉发间？祖国，
远方，你瞧，一只螳螂在赶贴标语
死人中也包括那曾在慢镜头里
喊不出声的
球门员。吹熄生日蜡烛的那当儿
有人说：“送你一个处女跳的芭蕾舞”
伞。在角隅，被薄膜裹紧一直未
开封。这儿，这乌有之乡，该有一片雨景
撑开吧。生活啊，快递给我的手

1992

Umbrella

Many words
Many words, never my destiny
Many shadows I cannot ride into winter
I won't end up as a rebel in this life
but who knows—I was enjoying a cold wind on the summit one day
hoping to stand on tiptoe, touch the kite's leaping heart
I was deserted. Played chess with myself
and turned mad. I long to be
an idle periscope suffocating in a submarine
When others die I'd rather be a ferryman
somewhere, deepest and deepest, landscape as before
How many dimensions are there, what
chimney smoke drifts between my eyebrows? Homeland,
look, a praying mantis is busy putting up posters
Among the dead in slow motion
a goalkeeper unable
to yell. Blowing out birthday candles
someone says, *Here is a gift, a ballet by a virgin*
Umbrella. In a corner, tightly wrapped and sealed
by a thin film all this while. Here, in this neverland, a rainscape must be
opening. O life, a hand delivered to me swiftly

1992

夜半的面包

十月已过，我并没有发疯
窗外的迷雾婴儿般滚动
我一生等待的唯一结果

未露端倪。如果我是寂静
那么隔着外套，面包也会来吃我

是谁派遣了这面包
那少年是我，把自行车颠倒在地
当他的手死命地摇转脚蹬
我便大吃那飞轮如水的肌肉

是谁派遣了灾难，派遣了辩证法
事物鸡零狗碎的上空
死人的眼睛含满棉花

我会吃自己，如果我是沉默

1992

Midnight Bread

October past, I'm not mad
Fog rolls outside the window like a baby
The one and only ending I await all my life

has yet to arrive. Were I stillness
even with a coat, bread would eat me too

Who has sent this bread
I am the boy, my bicycle reversed on the floor
When he violently rotates the pedal with his hands
I devour the watery flywheel flesh

Who sends disaster and dialectics
Odds and ends in the air
Dead eyes full of cotton

Were I silence, I would eat myself

1992

哀歌

一封信打开有人说
天已凉
另一封信打开
是空的，是空的
却比世界沉重
一封信打开
有人说他在登高放歌
有人说，不，即便死了
那土豆里活着的惯性
还会长出小手呢
另一封信打开
你熟睡如橘
但有人剥开你的赤裸后说
他摸到了另一个你
另一封信打开
他们都在大笑
周身之物皆暴笑不已
一封信打开
行云流水在户外猖獗
一封信打开
我咀嚼着某些黑暗
另一封信打开
皓月当空
另一封信打开后喊
死，是一件真事情

1992

Elegy

a letter opens and someone says
it's getting cold
another letter opens
it is empty, empty
yet heavier than the world
a letter opens
someone says he is singing from a mountain height
someone says *no, even if the potato were dead*
the inertia alive in it
would still grow tiny hands
another letter opens
you sleep like a tangerine
but after peeling you bare someone says
he has touched another you
another letter opens
they are all laughing
everything around explodes into laughter
a letter opens
clouds and water run wild outside
a letter opens
I am chewing a certain darkness
another letter opens
high moon in the sky
another letter opens and shouts
death is something real

1992

护身符

如果你真愿佩戴
它就是护身符
它扑朔迷离，它会从
那机器刨出的小小木葫芦
以檀香油的方式
越狱似地打出一拳

“不”这个词，挂在树上
如果你愿意
“不”也会流泪，鳄鱼一样
护身符的某日啊
月亮正分娩月亮
凌驾于一切表达之上

树在落发
抽屉打开如舌头
如果你愿意，护身符便是那
疼得钻进你脑袋中的
灯泡，它阿谀世上的黑暗

灯的普照下，一切恍若来世
事物宽恕了自己还不是自己
宽恕了所窃踞位置的空洞
“不”这个词，驮走了你的肉体
“不”这个护身符，左右开弓
你躬身去解鞋带的死结
你掩耳盗铃。旷野——
不！不！不！

1992

Talisman

If you are truly willing to wear it
it will be a talisman
Unfathomable and complex, from
an industrial wooden gourd
it will thrust a fist with sandalwood oil
as if to break out of jail

The word *No* hangs on the tree
If you are willing
No can shed tears like a crocodile
O someday in the life of the talisman
the moon is giving birth to the moon
soaring above all expressions

Trees shave their hair
Drawers open like tongues
If you are willing, the talisman can become
a light bulb so painful it drills into your
brain, it flatters darkness in the world

Under a bright lamp, as if in an afterlife
all things had forgiven the self that wasn't itself
and the void that usurped position
The word *No* carries away your body
The talisman *No* draws its bow left and right
You bend to untie a dead knot on a shoelace
You are a cat that shuts its eyes while stealing cream. Wilderness—
No! No! No!

1992

今年的云雀

但最末一根食指独立于手
但叶子找不到树
但干涸的不是田野中的乐器
总之它们不是运载信息
这是一支空白练习曲
　　“首先是敲，如盲人恓惶于生门前
　　但不似药片的那种敲
　　因为不屑于吻合
　　不吻合于某种臆想
　　不以融解你我为最佳理想
　　是敲，但敲只敲那种形象
　　像你打开自己还是自己
　　短暂打开后还是短暂
　　敲是回家？
　　但家不该含有羞怯和尴尬
　　但家应该是这儿，这儿
　　随喊随开。敲。”
　　　　　　　　然后谁也猜不透
你这云雀葬身何方。我站起
我摸到快结霜的天气里
无边无限的墙
我给它的空空如也戴上一副墨镜
仿佛是随手画到一张白纸上
红色单薄的墨镜表示寻人
而迷途的人儿拾到一只死鸟

1993

The Lark This Year

But the last index finger is independent of the hand
But the leaves can't find the trees
But what shrivels are not the musical instruments in the fields
In short they carry no message
This is a blank *étude*
        "First, knock—like a restless blind man before an obscure gate
        but unlike the knock of a tablet
        for it disdains coincidence
        unfit for some conjecture
        does not uphold *melting into each other* as the ideal
        Knock, but just knock at that image
        the way you knock open yourself and remain yourself
        brevity opens and remains brevity
        Is to knock to go home?
        But home shouldn't hold shyness and embarrassment
        But home should be here, here
        Doors will open at your shout. Knock."
                                        No one can guess
where you, lark, are buried. I stand up
In the soon-frosted weather I feel
the boundless wall
I put a pair of sunglasses on its void
as if casually drawing onto a blank paper
Red, flimsy sunglasses indicate a search for the missing
while the one lost in his way finds a dead bird

1993

祖父

鸣蝉的脚踏车尾夹紧几副秘方，
门虚掩着，我写作的某个午晌。
祖父泪滴的拳头最后一次松开——
纸条落空：明天会特别疼痛；

因为脱臼者是无力回天的，逝者也
无需大地；幽灵用电热丝发明着
沸腾，嗲声嗲气的欢迎，对这
生的，冷的人境唱喏对不起；

南风的脚踏车闻着有远人的气息，
桐影多姿，青风啄食吐香的珠粒；
摇响车铃的刹那间，尾随的广场
突然升空，芸芸众生惊呼，他们

第一次在右上方看见微茫的自身
脱落原地，口中哇吐几只悖论的
风筝。隔着晴朗，祖父身穿中山装
降落，字迹的清晰度无限放大，

他回到身外一只缺口的碗里，用
盐的滋味责怪我：写，不及读；
诀别之际，不如去那片桃花潭水
踏岸而歌，像汪伦，他的新知己；
读，远非做，但读懂了你也就做了。

Grandpa

A bicycle of droning cicadas is clamped with secret prescriptions,
door unlocked, I write at noon.
Grandpa loosens his grip with tears for the last time—
a slip of paper falls: tomorrow will particularly hurt;

because dislocated men can't save the day, the dead
need no universe; ghosts invent boiling with heating
wire as their childish welcome, a polite
apology for this cold, unfamiliar human world;

the bicycle of south wind smells of the breath of estranged men,
graceful shadows of paulownias, young phoenixes peck at fragrant peaberries;
precisely when the bicycle bell rings, the square behind
suddenly rises, the masses exclaim, for the first time they

see their hazy selves drop from where they were
at the top right, their mouths puffing out kites
of paradox. Apart from a bright day, Grandpa lands in a Chinese
tunic, the legibility of his handwriting grows infinitely,

he returns to a chipped bowl outside his body, reprimands
me with the taste of salt: reading is writing;
upon parting, why not go to the pond of peach blossoms,
rejoice and sing once ashore, like Wang Lun, his new bosom friend;
reading is far from action, but once you have read it you have done something.

你果真做了，上下四方因迷狂的
节拍而温暖和开阔，你就写了；
然后便是临风骋望，像汪伦。写，

为了那缭绕于人的种种告别。

1994

Indeed you have done so, the space warms up, broadening
in all directions from a furious beat, so you write;
à la Wang Lun, gaze afar with the wind. Write

for various farewells lingering above men.

1994

而立之年

一边哭泣一边干着眼下的活儿
自由，燕子一般，离开了铁锤
我的十根手指纳闷地伸向土地的尽头
聆听。是什么声音呀，找着，找着
一种旋律，一块可以藏身伏虎的大圆石
一个迹象，一柄快剑，让我学习忍受自己
雨意正浓，前人手捧一把山茱萸在峰顶走动
他向我演绎一条花蛇，一技之长，皮可不存
关键有脱落后的盈腴，鸣响沧海桑田的可能
歌者必忧；槐树下，西风和晚餐边一台凋败的水泵
在那里，刺绣出深情的母龙的身体
要走多少路，人才能看见桌上的一只
鳄梨啊？周围是
一杯红酒，一颗止痛片，口琴，落扣，英雄牌
金笔，它们都偎着我朴素的中年取暖
我身上的逝者谈到下一次爱情时
试探地将两把亮匙贴卧在一起，头靠紧头
是什么声音呢，哑默地躲在
日常之神的磁场里？
燕子自由地离开铁锤
外面正越缩越小，直到雷电中最末一个邮递员
呐喊着我的名字奔来，再也不能转身出去
玻璃窗上的裂缝
铺开一条幽深的地铁，我乘着它驶向神迹，或
中途换车，上升到城市空虚的中心，狂欢节
正热闹开来：我呀我呀连同糟糕的我呀
抛撒，倾斜，蹦跳，非花非雾。高脚杯突然

At Thirty

Weeping and finishing the task at hand
free like swallows, leaving the hammer
Stretched to the ends of the soil, my ten fingers wonder
and listen. What sound is it—searching, searching
for a melody, a boulder where men and tigers hide
a sign, a swift épée, so I learn to endure myself
Dense rain, someone in front moves around the summit holding dogwood
and infers a colorful snake, a unique skill, its skin nowhere
Still it looks plump after its skin shed, hissing the possible transformation
A singer disquiets; under a pagoda tree, a ruined water pump along the west
wind and dinner
where the tender body of a dragoness is embroidered
How far must one walk to see the avocado
on the table? Surrounded
by a glass of red wine, a painkiller, a harmonica, a fallen button, a Hero
fountain pen in gold—they snuggle up and bask in the warmth of my plain
middle age
When the dead on my body evokes the next love
trying to stick two shiny spoons together, head against head—
what sound is it, hidden quietly within a
magnetic field of everyday gods?
Swallows leave the hammer freely
The outside world shrinks until the last postman comes rushing
in the storm yelling my name, unable to turn around and exit
Cracks in the window glass
pave the way for a deep calm subway. I take a ride to miracle, or
transfer midway, rising to the empty city center, the carnival
bustling and on its way: oh I oh I and the terrible me
scattered, tipped, leaping, neither fog nor flower. Suddenly the wine glass

摔碎，它里面的那匹骏马戛止
如一绺高贵香水
于黑暗中循循诱动
我祷告的笔正等着我志在四方的真实儿女，而
一种对公社秧苗的
不详预感
一种谈心，无法践约的
在我之外，如一个滑旱冰的
小阿飞
委蛇而来。

1994

falls into pieces, the stallion inside comes to an abrupt halt
like a waft of noble perfume
seducing me steadily in the dark
My pen in prayer is waiting for my real aspiring children, while
                                                                                                    a foreboding
                                                                        about communal plants
like a heart-to-heart talk, unable to honor its promise
something beyond me, like a roller-skating
                                                                                                              punk
who meanders here with the snake.

1994

跟茨维塔伊娃的对话
（十四行组诗）

C'est un Chinois, ce sera long.
—Marina Tsvetajeva

1

亲热的黑眼睛对你露出微笑，
我向你兜售一只绣花荷包，
翠青的表面，凤凰多么小巧，
金丝绒绣着一个“喜”字的吉兆——
两个？Nyet，两个半法郎。你看，
半个之差会带来一个坏韵，
像我们走出人行道，分行路畔
你再听不懂我的南方口音；
等红绿灯变成一个绿色幽人，
你继续向左，我呢，蹀躞向右。
不是我，却突然像我，某人
头发飞逝向你跑来，举着手，

某种东西，不是花，却花一样
递到你悄声细语的剧院包厢。

Dialogue with Tsvetaeva
[a sequence of sonnets]

It's a Chinese, it will be long.
—Marina Tsvetaeva

1

My dark eyes smile at you with affection.
I am trying to sell you an embroidered pouch,
crisp green, such an exquisite phoenix.
Joy, an auspicious word stitched in golden silk—
Two? *Nyet*, two and a half francs. Look,
the difference of half a franc is a false rhyme,
like us stepping off the sidewalk on our separate ways.
Again, you don't get my Southern accent;
waiting for traffic lights to turn into a green recluse,
you keep turning left, I take small steps to the right.
Not me but someone else looking suddenly like me,
hair flying, running to you, one hand raised,

something, not a flower, but flowery,
sent to the theater box of your whisper.

2

我天天梦见万古愁。白云悠悠，
玛琳娜，你煮沸一壶私人咖啡，
方糖迢递地在蓝色近视外愧疚
如一个僮仆。他向往大是大非。
诗，干着活儿，如手艺，其结果
是一件件静物，对称于人之境，
或许可用？但其分寸不会超过
两端影子恋爱的括弧。圆手镜
亦能诗，如果谁愿意，可他得
防备它错乱右翼和左边的习惯，
两个正面相对，翻脸反目，而
红与白因“不”字决斗；人，迷惘，

照镜，革命的僮仆从原路返回；
砸碎，人兀然空荡，咖啡惊坠……

2

Every day I dream of eternal sorrow. Clouds drifting,
Marina, you brew a pot of coffee in private,
lump sugar far beyond the near vision of blue, guilty
like a houseboy. He looks forward to major issues.
Poetry, like a craft, to labor, the result
a series of still lifes, human plights in symmetry,
might it serve? Yet its limits can't surpass
brackets loved by two shadows. A round hand mirror
also knows poetry, should someone wish, but he must
guard against its habit of muddling right and left wings,
two fronts facing each other, fallen out, while
red and white duel over *No*; man, in a maze,

looking into the mirror, the houseboy of revolution is backtracking;
pulverized, one suddenly feels empty, the coffee falls in shock . . .

3

……我照旧将头埋进空杯里面；
你完蛋了，未来一边找葬礼服，
一边用绷紧的零碎打发下午，
俄罗斯完蛋了——黑白时代的底片，
男低音：您早，清脆的高中生：
啊——走吧——进来呀——哭就哭——好吗？
尊称的面具舞会，代词后颤“R”
马达般转动着密约桦林和红吻。
巴黎也完蛋了，
　　　　　　　　我落座一柄阳伞下
张望和工作。人在搭构新书库，
四边是四座象征经典的高楼，
中间镶嵌花园和玻璃阅读架。

人，完蛋了，如果词的传诵，
不像蝴蝶，将花的血脉震悚

3

. . . as usual, I bury my head in an empty glass;
you're finished, the future is looking for burial clothes
and sending off an afternoon with taut fragments.
Russia is finished—the negatives of a black-and-white era.
A male bass: *Bonjour.* The melodious voice of a high school student:
Ah—Go—Come—Just cry—All right?
Masquerade of honorific titles, an *R* trembles behind the pronoun.
Like a motor it rotates birches and red kisses from a secret rendezvous.
Paris is finished too.
                                        Sitting under a parasol,
I look around and work. Men are building a new *bibliothèque*,
surrounded by four canonical towers,
a garden and glass bookstands embedded in the center.

Man, now finished—should the afterlife of words,
unlike butterflies, terrify a flower's veins.

4

我们的睫毛，为何在异乡跳跃?
慌惑，溃散，难以投入形象。
母语之舟撇弃在汪洋的边界，
登岸，我徒步在我之外，信箱
打开如特洛伊木马，空白之词
蜂涌，给清晨蒙上萧杀的寒霜;
陌生，在煤气灶台舞动蛇腰子，
流亡的残月散发你月经的辛酸，
妈妈，卡珊德拉，专业的预言家，
他们逼着你的侧影吸外国烟，
而阳光，仍舒展它最糟糕的惩罚:
鸟越精确，人越不当真，虽然

火中的一页纸咿呀，飒飒消失，
真相之魂夭逃——灰烬即历史。

4

Our eyelashes—why do they leap in a foreign land?
Frantic, in defeat, hard to plunge into image.
Boat of the mother tongue, abandoned at sea's edge.
Ashore, I set foot beyond myself, the mailbox
opens like a Trojan horse, empty words
like a swarm of bees, a shroud of bleak frost at morning;
the uncanny twirls a snake kidney on a gas stove,
waning moon of exile disperses your menstrual pain.
Mother, Cassandra, the professional prophet,
they force your silhouette to smoke imported cigarettes.
Sunlight, unfolding its worst punishment:
the more precise the birds, the more serious we aren't, though

a sheet of paper squeaks in fire, vanishes in a swish,
the soul of truth fleeing—ashes, history.

5

阳光偶尔也会是一只狼，遍地
转悠，影子含着回忆的橄榄核，
那是神，叫你的嘴回味他色情的
津沫，让你失灵，预言之盒
无力装运行尸走肉，沐浴在
这被耀眼的盲目所统辖的沙滩。
看见即说出，而说出正是大海，
此刻的。圆。看的羊癫疯。看。

生活，在哪？“赫克托，我看见你
坐着一万双眼睛里抽泣，发愣”——
你站在这，但尸体早发白。等你
再回到外面，英雄早隐身，只剩

非人和可乐瓶，围观肌肉的健美赛，
龙虾般生猛的零件，凸现出未来。

5

Sunlight is occasionally a wolf, sauntering
across the land, a shadow sucks on an olive pit of memory.
It's God who plants in your mouth the aftertaste
of His foamy eroticism and makes you impotent, the box of prophecy
powerless to cart away walking corpses, bathing
on the shore governed by dazzling blindness.
To see is to speak. And *sea* is the word spoken
at this instant. A circle. Look at epilepsy. Look.

Where is life? *Hector, I saw you*
sobbing, transfixed in ten thousand pairs of eyes—
here you stand, the corpse has turned ashen. When you
return to the world, the hero is long unseen, leaving behind

nonhumans and Coke bottles, crowding to watch a bodybuilding contest,
the future protruding from spare parts, as vigorous as lobsters.

6

樱桃，红艳艳的，像在等谁归来。
某种东西，我想去取。下午，
我坐着坐着就睡了，耳朵也倦怠，
我答应去外地取回一本俄文书。
你坐在你散发里，云雀是帽子。
笔，因寻找而温暖。远方，来客。
梦寐之中，你的手滴落着断指，
我想去取：人，铜号，和火车；

樱桃，红艳艳的，等的纯粹逻辑，
我心跳地估算自己所剩的时光；
没有你，祖国之窗多空虚。呼吸，
我去取，生词像鲟鱼领你还乡；

你去取，门锁里小无赖哇吐静电——
痛，但合唱惊警地凌空，绝缘。

6

Cherries, a scarlet red, as if waiting for someone to return.
Something I'd like to fetch. Afternoon,
dozing off as I sit and sit, even ears grow bored.
I promise to bring home a Russian book.
You sit in your loose hair, a lark for a hat.
A pen feels warm because it is sought. A guest from afar.
In a dream your hand drips with severed fingers,
I'd like to fetch people, a brass trumpet, a train;

cherries, a scarlet red, the pure logic of waiting,
my heart flutters and counts my time left;
without you, how empty the window of homeland. Breathe,
I'll fetch new words to lead you home like sturgeon.

Go fetch them. A little rascal spews static in the door lock—
it hurts, but the choir soars in alarm, insulated.

7

你回到莫斯科，碰了个冷钉子，
而生活的踉跄正是诗歌的踉跄。
除夕夜，乌鸦的儿女衣冠楚楚地
等钟声，而时间坏了，只好四散。
带担架的风景里躺着那总机员，
作协的电话空响：现实又迟到，
这人死了，那人疯了，抱怨，
抱怨的长脚蚊摇响空袭警报。
完美啊完美，你总是忍受一个
既短暂又字正腔圆的顶头上司，
一个句读的哈巴儿，一会说这
长了点儿，一会说你思想还幼稚，

楼顶的同行，事后报火，他们
跛足来贺，来尝尝你死的闭门羹。

7

Back in Moscow, you suffer an icy rebuff.
Staggering life, staggering poetry.
On New Year's Eve, the dainty children of crows
wait for bells to toll. Time isn't working, they disperse.
In the scenery with a stretcher lies the phone operator.
The Writers' Union telephone rings in vain: *Reality is late again,*
this man is dead, that man is mad, complaint after complaint,
a crane fly complains and sets off the air-raid siren.
O perfection, you always put up with an
interim director whose clear articulation
sounds like a Pekingese—*This is a bit*
long or *You're quite naïve.*

Rooftop compatriots yell *Fire* after the incident, limping
to congratulate you, tasting the cold shoulder of your death.

8

> Wenn Duwirdlich mich sechen willst,
> so musst Du handeln!
>
> —Tsvetaeva an Rilke

东方既白，经典的一幕正收场：
俩知音一左一右，亦人亦鬼，
谈心的橘子荡漾着言说的芬芳，
深处是爱，恬静和肉体的玫瑰。
手艺是触摸，无论你隔得多远；
你的住址名叫不可能的可能——
你轻轻说着这些，当我祈愿
在晨风中送你到你焚烧的家门：
词，不是物，这点必须搞清楚，
因而首先得生活有趣的生活，
像此刻——木兰花盎然独立，倾诉，
警报解除，如情人的发丝飘落。

东方既白，你在你名字里失踪，
植树的众鸟齐唱：注意天空。

8

If you really want to see me, you have to act!
—Tsvetaeva to Rilke

Dawn in the east. A classic scene comes to an end.
Two soulmates, left and right, half-human, half-ghost.
Talking heart to heart, tangerines undulate with the aroma of speech.
Deep inside is love, the rose of tranquility and flesh.
However distant you are, a touch is a skill.
Your address is the name of the impossible possibility—
softly you speak of this as I pray
to send you back on a morning breeze to your burning doorstep:
a word is not an object—this must be made clear,
so one must first live an interesting life
like at this instant—lush magnolia blooms stand on their own, pouring out their woes.
The siren stops like a lover's hair floating to the ground.

Dawn in the east. You've gone missing from your name.
Birds from the woods sing in unison, *Beware the sky*.

9

人周围的事物，人并不能解释；
为何可见的刀片会夺走魂灵？
两者有何关系？绳索，鹅卵石，
自己，每件小东西，皆能索命，
人造的世界，是个纯粹的敌人，
空缺的花影愤怒地喝彩四壁，
使你害怕，我常常想，不是人
更不是你本身，勾销了你的形体；
而是这些弹簧般的物品，窜出，
整个封杀了眼睛的居所，逼迫
你喊：外面啊外面，总在别处！
甚至死也只是衔接了这场漂泊。

无根的电梯，谁上下玩弄着按钮？
我最怕自己是自己唯一的出口。

9

People can't explain everything around them —
how can a visible razor blade seize a soul?
How are they related? Rope, cobblestone,
self, each tiny thing can claim a life.
The man-made world, a pure enemy.
Empty flower shadows cheer four walls in fury,
frightening you. Often I think, it is not man
nor even yourself who delete your form,
but these objects, darting out like coil springs,
blacklist the eyes of the entire dwelling, forcing
you to yell: *Outside, outside, always somewhere else!*
Even death is merely linking up this wandering.

Rootless elevator, who is fooling with the buttons?
I am my only exit—this is what I fear most.

10

我摘下眼镜，我愿是聋哑人的翻译——
宇宙的孩子们，大厅正鸦雀无声：
空气朗读着这首诗，它的含义
被手势的蝴蝶催促开花的可能。
真实的底蕴是那虚构的另一个，
他不在此地，这月亮的对应者，
不在乡间酒吧，像现在没有我——
一杯酒被匿名地啜饮着，而景色
的格局竟为之一变。满载着时空，
饮酒者过桥，他愕然回望自己
仍滞留对岸，满口吟哦。某种
悲天悯人的情怀，和变革之计
使他的步伐配制出世界的轻盈。
大人先生，你瞧，遍地的月影……

10

Taking off my eyeglasses, I wish to translate for the deaf and the mute—
children of the universe, silence reigns in the hall:
air is reciting this poem, its meaning the chance
of blossoms coaxed by the gestures of butterflies.
The interior details of reality is the fictive other.
He isn't here, the equivalent of the moon,
not in a village bar, like now, without me—
a glass of wine sipped anonymously, the landscape
structure changes abruptly. Laden with time and space,
the drinker crosses the bridge, stunned in self-retrospection,
Reciting poetry, he lingers on the other bank. Bemoaning
the fate of mankind, reform plans
orchestrate the lightness of this world from his footsteps.
Sir, look—moon shadows everywhere . . .

11

……是的，大人，月亮扑面而起，
四望皎然，峰顶紧贴着你腮鬓：
下面，城南的路灯吐露香皂气，
生活的她夜半淋浴，双眼闭紧，
窗纱呢喃手影，她洗发如祈祷，
回身隐入黑暗，冰箱亮开一下；
永恒像野猫，广告美男子踅到
彗星外，冰淇淋天空满是俏皮话……
……夜莺啊正在别处，是的，您瞧，
没在弹钢琴的人，也在弹奏，
无家可归的人，总是在回家：
不多不少，正好应合了万古愁——
呵大人，告诉我，为何没有的桂树
卷入心思，振奋了夜的秩序？

11

. . . yes, sir, the moon surges.
Snow everywhere, mountain peaks stick to your sideburns:
below, streetlamps south of the city exude a scent of perfumed soap.
In life she showers at midnight with her eyes shut,
curtains murmur in hand shadows, she washes her hair like in a prayer,
turns around, hidden in the dark, the fridge opens with a glow;
eternity like a wild cat, handsome men from the ads walk
beyond the comet, jokes and quips fill the ice-cream sky . . .
. . . O the nightingale is elsewhere now, yes, sir, look,
the one who isn't playing the piano also performs,
the homeless are always going home:
no more, no less, just right for eternal sorrow—
O sir, tell me, why isn't there a cassia tree
drawn into thoughts to uplift the order of night?

12

九月，果真会有一场告别？
你的目光，摆设某个新室内：
小铜像这样，转椅那样，落叶，
这清凉宇宙的女友，无畏：
对吗，对吗？睫毛的合唱追问，
此刻各自的位置，真的对吗？
王，掉落在棋局之外；西风
将云朵的银行广场吹到窗下：
正午，各自的人，来到快餐亭，
手指朝着口描绘面包的通道；
对吗，诗这样，流浪汉手风琴
那样？丰收的喀秋莎把我引到
我正在的地点：全世界的脚步，
暂停！对吗？该怎样说：“不”！？

1994

12

Will there really be a September farewell?
Your gaze furnishes and decorates a new interior;
this bronze statue, that swivel chair, fallen leaves,
this cool cosmos, its fearless girlfriend:
Yes, yes? A chorus of eyelashes interrogates,
Is everyone in the right place right now?
The king drops out of a chess game; a west wind
blows the clouds and their bank plaza under the window:
at noon, each individual comes to the fast-food booth,
a finger pointing to the mouth, depicting a bread channel;
is this poetry, and that, the accordion
of a vagrant? The "Katyusha" of harvest leads me
to where I am: *Footsteps worldwide,*
halt! Yes? How do I say No?

1994

纽约夜眺

I will go to the bank by the wood and become undisguised and naked
—Walt Whitman

手捧红鳟鱼攀登暗夜
　纽约好比纽约，垂挂于
　　一滴热泪，飘向深渊

星相的心跳蟑螂般窜动
　脂肪中的防盗锁沿途
　　播种耳朵，宝石，逃脱

和你；挽着你的纽约王
　你漫步在第五大道上
　　幽魂车队递来迷迭香

有关体态之痛的故事
　全部屈服于眼影深处
　　但是，有什么比成功更

色情的呢？夜空飘来
　一朵彩云，来自永恒的
　　偶尔安慰，看不见的你

和阙如的纽约王走着
　未来酒吧镀金的内部
　　男女蝙蝠般吮吸着明镜

Nightview, New York

> I will go to the bank by the wood and become undisguised and naked
> —Walt Whitman

Holding a red trout you scale the dark night
New York is just New York, dangling
in a hot teardrop, drifting to an abyss

The zodiac heartbeat scurries like a cockroach
An anti-theft lock embedded in fat
sowing along ears, gems, evasion

and you; arm in arm with the King of New York
you stroll down Fifth Avenue
Ghostly cars hand out rosemaries

Stories about the pains of posture
yield to the depth of eye shadows
But what is more erotic than

success? In the night sky
floats a cloud, from eternity
a sporadic consolation, the unseen you

walks with the defected King of New York
Within the gilt interior of a future pub
men and women suck a bright mirror like bats

你用打火机招来火焰的
　一朵，侍者之水鞠躬
　　历史的烟头一时找不着

左边或右边，便随手弹进
　第三世界的烟灰缸里
　　半个情人余音袅袅

吻另半个，西维娅·普拉斯
　她多么骄傲地憎恨赤裸
　　整体好比一颗生洋葱

剥到中心，只见哭泣的皮
　分解成旋转门，杀手路过
　　你难以脱身，像世界穿着

地铁的内裤停也停不下来
　死神，这铬钢的剪票员
　　下流地挡路，一个接一个

手捧红鳟鱼走进暗夜
　你追踪你最知心的密友
　　一个有着易性癖的多梦者——

磁铁的舞妹，诺言的蒙娜丽莎，
　脸上荡漾着悠远的神情
　　身上，帝国客观的粘黏物

被她舞落，飞溅于乌有乡
　异想天开的身份之谜
　　神经里经营着灯红酒绿

With a lighter you provoke a petal
of flame, the waiter bows with his water
a cigarette butt of history lost for now

Left or right, just flick it into
an ashtray from the Third World
Like lingering smoke, you the half-lover

kiss the other half-lover, Sylvia Plath
How proud she is, she who hates nudity
The whole is like a raw onion

peeled to its heart, see how the weeping skin
splits into revolving doors, an assassin passes
You can't escape, like the world in

a metro's underwear, no way to stop
Azrael, a ticket inspector in chrome steel
blocks the way, vulgarly, one after another

Holding a red trout you walk into dark night
tracking down your closest soulmate
a dreamer suffering from transsexualism—

a magnetic sing-song girl, the Mona Lisa of promises
a long-ago look rippling across her face
On her body, an objective sticker of the empire

danced away, splattering upon a never-never-land
the wildest riddle of identity
Debauchery runs a business in the nerves

她怎能觉察你这娉婷的
解放者，进来，露天消失
零星的外面抛赏给自杀者

他下坠，仿真，下落不明
或无恙，被大拇指，遥控器上
的瘾君子劫向图片的海绵垫

电视机，幸免者思想的批发站
里面那副 Tarot 扑克
正一一亮牌，请人认领

换牌：一个教师模样的
尴尬人，正预言似的突破
那法语字谜：鱼，Poisson

“若漏掉当中的一个s
就成了毒品”，纽约王心想，
“怪不得巴黎人吃鱼考究”

“我这就去那葱茏的堤岸
去那儿袒露体魄和真容”
但世界能否好转？可能的

惠特曼，哼着这自己之歌
驾驶幽灵中最短暂的出租车
运着几个落魄的卫星人

从布鲁克林大桥上经过——
乌云正给男式摩天大楼
戴上呢帽，天使们擦窗

How can she notice you, graceful
liberator, come—the open air disappears
Fragments from beyond, a reward for a suicide

And he falls, a simulator, nowhere to be found
or safe and sound, seized by a thumb, an addict hooked
to a remote control, into images of a foam cushion

TV, the distributor of survival thoughts
Inside, Tarot cards are laid
out one by one, asking to be claimed

and replaced: embarrassed, a man who looks
like a teacher breaks through prophetically
a French riddle: fish, *poisson*

If an "s" is dropped
it'll become "poison," the King of New York tells himself
No wonder Parisians are such picky fish eaters

I will go to the bank by the wood
and become undisguised and naked
Will the world change for the better? Possibly

Whitman is humming this "Song of Myself"
driving among ghosts the most transient cab
with some down-and-out aliens

Crossing the Brooklyn Bridge—
dark clouds put felt hats on manly
skyscrapers, angels scrub windows

从布鲁克林大桥上经过——
　后视镜看见你七窍出血
　　被几个黑影长久地，必然地

殴打着。你站着，平静地注视
　哪儿，哪儿是我的缪斯啊？
　　爱着，忍着，问着，我

手捧红鳟鱼深入暗夜
　你口含一泓沁泉，开放了
　　雕像上空破晓的为什么

1994

Crossing the Brooklyn Bridge—
in a rear-view mirror, I see blood ooze from seven orifices
beaten up by dark shadows, inevitably

and for a long time. You stand and watch calmly
Where, where is my Muse?
To love, to endure, to question—I

hold a red trout deep into the dark night
a spring in your mouth, opening up
the *why* of first light above a statue

1994

厨师

未来是一阵冷颤从体内搜刮
而过，翻倒的醋瓶渗透筋骨。
厨师推门，看见黄昏像一个小女孩，
正用舌尖四处摸找着灯的开关。
室内有着一个孔雀一样的具体，
天花板上几个气球，还活着一种活：
厨师忍住突然。他把豆腐一分为二，
又切成小寸片，放进鼓掌的油锅，
煎成金黄的双面；
　　　　　　　　再换另一个锅，
煎香些许姜末肉泥和红艳的豆瓣，
汇入豆腐；再添点黄酒味精清水，
令其被吸入内部而成为软的奥妙；
现在，撒些青白葱丁即可盛盘啦。
厨师因某个梦而发明了这个现实，
户外大雪纷飞，在找着一个名字。
从他痛牙的深处，天空正慢慢地
把那小花裙抽走。
从近视镜片，往事如精液向外溢出。
　　　　　　　　厨师极端地把
头颅伸到窗外，菜谱冻成了一座桥，
通向死不相认的田野。他听呀听呀：
果真，有人在做这道菜，并把
这香喷喷的诱饵摆进暗夜的后院。
有两声“不”字奔走在时代的虚构中，
像两个舌头的小野兽，冒着热气
在冰封的河面，扭打成一团……

1995

Chef

The future is a chill clawing its way out from the inner
body. Spilled vinegar penetrates muscle and bone.
The chef pushes open the door, sees twilight like a girl,
feeling for a light switch with the tip of her tongue.
Inside, something as concrete as a peacock,
balloons on the ceiling still with some life:
the chef holds back the surprise. He slices the tofu in two,
then into smaller pieces, drops them in the applauding wok of oil,
fries them until they turn golden on both sides;
                                                            next, with another wok,
he pan-fries minced ginger and meat in a crimson bean paste,
mixes them with the tofu, adds a dash of yellow wine, MSG, and water,
letting them soak into a soft marvel.
Now, sprinkle some diced green onions and it's ready to serve.
Because of a dream, the chef invents this reality,
snow whirling outside, seeking a name.
Deep in his aching tooth, the sky slowly
withdraws a floral skirt.
Through myopic lenses, the past seeps out like sperm.
                                              Exceedingly the chef
stretches his head from the window, the recipe freezes into a bridge,
leading to the fields that disown the bridge. He listens and listens:
indeed, someone else is making this dish, placing
this savory bait in the backyard of the dark night.
Twice the word *No* runs in the fiction of the era,
like two small-tongued beasts puffing out hot air
on a frozen river, wrestling with each other . . .

1995

祖国

已经夜半了，南方阴冷之香叫你
抱头跪下来，幽蓝渗透的空车厢停下
等信号，而新年还差几分钟才送你到站。
梅树上你瞥见一窝灯火，叽叽喳喳的，
家与家之间，正用酒杯摆设多少个
　　　　　　　　　环环相扣的圆圈。
你跳进郊野，泥泞在脚下叫你的绰号，
你连声答应着，呵气像一件件破陶器。
夜，漏着雪片，你眼睛不知该如何
看。真的空无一人吗？
　　　　　　　　　　冷像一匹
锐亮的缎子被忍了十年的四周抖了出来，
倾泻在田埂上命令你喝它。
　　　　　　突然，第一朵焰火
　　　　　　　　　砰上了天，像美人儿
对你说好吧。
　　　　　　　　　青春作伴，第二朵
更响。你呼啸："弟弟！弟弟！"——
天上的回响变幻着佼佼者的发型。
这时火车头也吼了几声，一绺蒸气托出
几只盘子和苹果，飞着飞着猛扑地，
穿你而过，挥着手帕，
　　　　　　　　　　像祖父没说完的话。
你猜那是说：回来啦，从小事做起吧。
乘警一惊，看见你野人般跳回车上来。

1996

Homeland

Already midnight and the bleak southern fragrance led you
to kneel down with your head buried, an empty coach seeped in a faint
blue paused
to wait for the signal, a few more minutes before New Year saw you off
to the station.
On a plum tree you caught a glimpse of a nest of lights chatting talkatively
among families, using wine glasses to display
interlocked circles.
You jumped into the country, mud under your feet called out your nickname.
You responded repeatedly, exhaling like broken pieces of earthenware.
Night, leaking with snowflakes, your eyes clueless about how
to look. Wasn't there a soul?
Cold like a skein
of shimmering satin unraveled after enduring a decade of its surroundings,
splattered on the ridge, ordering you to drink.
Suddenly, the first petal of fireworks
banged in the sky, like a beautiful woman
who told you *All right*.
Youth as companion, the second petal
a louder blast. You wailed, *Brother! Brother!—*
Echoes in the sky transformed into the hairstyles of prominent figures.
At this moment, a locomotive howled several times, a wisp of steam served
some plates and apples flew in a swoop
through and past you, waving a handkerchief
like Grandpa's unfinished words.
You guessed that they meant *Come back and start small.*
Taken aback, the railway policeman saw you jump back onto the train like
a savage.

1996

献给 C. R. 的一片钥匙

万吨黑暗。我们回家，衣裳鼓满西风。
书架上一杯水被阻隔。
　　　　　　　　　　隐身于浩淼，燕子
正瞄准千里外一枚小分币迁飞，
我们却被锁在屋外山影的记忆里。
你的赤裸溢满廊台，
四周，黑磁铁之夜有如沉思者吸紧

空旷。钥匙吮着世界。
一封误投的航空信在你和我之间递来递去。
“大”，它低语，“大”，

火苗一跳：呵，信，无止境地长大，
它叮咛我们住进里面。
你大醉而哇吐，我琢磨着写回信，
我的投影拎着两片纸，仿佛
　　　　我在伸展我感激又畸形的翅翼。

1996

A Key Dedicated to C. R.

Ten thousand tons of dark. On our way home, clothes bloat with the
westerly wind.
A glass of water, isolated on the bookshelf.
Cloaked in the vastness, swallows
aim their migration at a one-cent coin a thousand miles beyond,
yet lock us in the memory of a mountain shadow outside the house.
The porch is brimming with your nakedness.
Around us, like *Le Penseur*, the black magnet of night absorbs

emptiness. The key sucks on the world.
By mistake, a letter *par avion* back and forth between us.
Big, it whispers. *Big*.

Tongues of flame leap—O letter, growing ad infinitum,
urges us to live inside its words.
You're drunk and throw up. I consider a reply,
my shadow carries two sheets of paper, like
stretching my grateful yet deformed wings.

1996

祖母

1

她的清晨，我在西边正憋着午夜。
她起床，叠好被子，去堤岸练仙鹤拳。
迷雾的翅膀激荡，河像一根傲骨
于冰封中收敛起一切不可见的仪典。
“空”，她冲天一唉，“而不止是
肉身，贯满了这些姿势”；她蓦地收功，
原型般凝定于一点，一个被发明的中心。

2

给那一切不可见的，注射一支共鸣剂，
以便地球上的窗户一齐敞开。

以便我端坐不倦，眼睛凑近
显微镜，逼视一个细胞里的众说纷纭
和它的螺旋体，那里面，谁正在头戴矿灯，
一层层挖向莫名的尽头。星星，
太空的胎儿，汇聚在耳鸣中，以便

物，膨胀，排他，又被眼睛切分成
原子，夸克和无穷尽？
　　　　　　　　　　以便这一幕本身
也演变成一个细胞，一个地球似的细胞，
搏动在那冥冥浩渺者的显微镜下：一个
母性的，湿腻的，被分泌的“O”；以便

Grandmother

1

Her early morning—I am in the West, suffocating at midnight.
She wakes up, makes her bed, goes to the riverbank to practice Magic
Crane Boxing.
Wings of mist stir, the river a proud bone
converging all of the unseen rituals in the frost.
Emptiness, she shrieks, *isn't merely about*
the body and flesh furnishing these postures. Suddenly she closes in,
back into a fixed model point, an invented center.

2

To all unseen, inject a dose of sympathy
for windows on the earth to open together.

For me to sit upright tirelessly, eyes move close
to a microscope, staring at divergent views in a cell
and its spiral body. Who's wearing a miner's lamp inside,
digging layer by layer into an unknown end? Stars,
fetuses in space, do they gather in tinnitus for

matter to expand and exclude, then split by eyes into
atoms, quarks, and infinity?
So that this scene
too evolves into a cell, a globe-like cell,
pulsating under the microscope of a man far, far away: a
maternal, sticky wet, secreted *O* for

室内满是星期三。
眼睛，脱离幻境，掠过桌面的金鱼缸
和灯影下暴君模样的套层玩偶，嵌入
夜之阑珊。

3

夜里的中午，春风猝起。我祖母
走在回居民点的路上，篮子满是青菜和蛋。
四周，吊车鹤立。忍着嬉笑的小偷翻窗而入，
去偷她的桃木匣子；
　　　　　　　　　　　他闯祸，以便与我们
对称成三个点，协调在某个突破之中。
圆。

1997

the room to be packed with Wednesdays.
Eyes, breaking from illusion, skim past a goldfish bowl on the table
matryoshka dolls, like tyrants under shadowed lights, embedded
in the waning night.

3

Nocturnal noon, a sudden spring wind. My grandmother
walks back to the neighborhood with a basket full of vegetables and eggs.
Cranes stand high around her. A thief stifles his giggles, enters from
                    a window
to steal her cherry wood box.
                    He creates havoc to form
three dots with us, harmonizing a breakthrough.
Circle.

1997

在森林中

1

几件你拖欠的事情，
乌云般把你叫到小山顶。
落叶的滑翔机，
远处几个跳伞的小问号蠕袅地落进
风景的瓶颈里。天气中似乎有谁在演算
一道数学题。
你焦灼。
钟声，钟声把一件无头的金铠甲
抛到森林的深处。那儿，雾
在秋风的边角运转着，启动
一个搁置的图像，
一个状如闹钟内部的温暖机房。
那儿，你走动。

2

你走动，似乎森林不在森林中。
松鼠如一个急迫的越洋电话劈开林径。
听着：出事了。
天空浮满故障，
一个广场倒扣了过来。
你挂下话筒，身上尽是枫叶。
蘑菇，把古铜色的螺钉拧得更紧——
使一家磁器店嵌入葱翠的自由大街，
使那些替死亡当侦探的影子
尾随进来。
他们瞥了瞥发票上的零，

In the Forest

1

A few outstanding issues
summon you like dark clouds to the hilltop.
A glider of falling leaves,
tiny question marks parachuting from afar, wriggling into
the bottleneck of scenery. In this weather someone seems to be working
out a math problem.
You feel anxious.
The bell strikes: each strike hurls a headless golden suit of armor
deep into the forest. There, fog
orbits in a corner of autumn wind, launching
a forsaken image,
a warm engine room shaped like the inside of an alarm clock.
There, you walk around.

2

You walk around as if the forest were not in the forest.
Like an urgent overseas phone call, a squirrel splits the forest path.
Listen: something's happened.
Failure floats in the sky,
a city square inverted.
You hang up the phone, maple leaves covering your body.
Mushrooms twist the bronze screws tighter—
embedding a china shop into the lush green Liberty Boulevard,
letting shadows who serve as death spies
trail in.
They glance at the zeros on the bill,

身子分成好几瓣踅出玻璃旋门。
他们向右拐，指了指
对岸的森林。
迷离的蝴蝶效应。
正午，流水吹着笛子。
磁器皎洁的表情，多姿的芭蕾舞。
它们说：砸吧。我们什么也不说。

3

你狂暴地走动。
那发票就攥在你手中，
你想去取回你那被典押的影子。
森林转暗，雨滴敲击着密叶的键盘，
你迷失。而
希望，总在左边。向左，
那儿，路标上一个哑默的抽象人
朝你点了点头；
绿，守候在树身里如母亲，
轻脆地拧着精确的齿条。
几只啄木鸟，边说边做，
一圈圈声波在时光中荡漾。
几只啄木鸟，充盈了整座森林，和
星期一。

4

一圈空地。
长跑者停在那儿修理他呼吸的器械。
他的干渴开放出满树的红苹果，
飘香升入金钟塔，归还或断送现实。

their bodies split into segments, a leg protruding from a revolving glass door.
They turn right, pointing
at the forest on the other shore.
Hazy butterfly effect.
At noon, running waters play the flute.
The crisp bright expression of porcelain, a ballet in varied poses.
They say, *Smash it. We won't say anything.*

3

You pace furiously.
Bill clutched in your hand,
wanting to retrieve your pawned shadow.
The forest darkens, raindrops striking the keyboard of dense leaves.
You are lost. But
hope is always on the left. To the left,
there, on the road sign, a mute abstract man
nods at you;
green, in a tree trunk, keeping watch like a mother,
twisting crisply a precise gear.
A few woodpeckers talk while working,
sound waves ripple in time, circle by circle.
A few woodpeckers permeate the entire forest and
Monday.

4

A circle of empty space.
A long-distance runner pauses to repair his breathing device.
His thirst opens a treeful of red apples.
The fragrance rises into a golden bell tower, returning or forfeiting reality.

他因干渴而深感孤独。他低头琢磨
他暖和的掌心：它仿佛是个火车站，
人声鼎沸。一群去郊游的孩子泼下几绺
缤纷的水柱。
光，派出一个酷似扳道工的影子站在岔道口。
他觉得他第一次从宇宙获得了双手，和
暴力。

1996. 11 图宾根

Because of his thirst, he feels a deep loneliness. He bows his head, ponders
his warm palm: a train station,
a babel of voices. A group of children on an outing splash in wisps
of dazzling water jets.
Light sends a switchman-like shadow to the crossroad.
For the first time he feels as if the universe had given him two hands and
violence.

November 1996, Tübingen

西湖梦

夜半，神仙呵斥着东边的小白驹。
一片茶叶在跳伞，染绿这杯水的肉身。
都举着靴子，人们骑在这星球上说谎。
从更高处看，西湖不过是一颗白尘。

美轮美奂，如果谁把这尘埃掏空又放大，
再倒进许多梦之绿。
西湖，三三两两的
逻辑从景点走了出来，像找回的零钱。
这不是真的。

而在你的城市定居的人，围拢你
像围拢一餐火锅。一条鲤鱼跃起，
给自己添一些醋。官员在风中，
响亮地抽着谁的耳光。
这也不是真的：

如果一滴泪呕吐出一大把鱼刺。
泪的分币花光了，而泪之外竟有一个
像那个西湖一样热泪盈眶的西湖，
黎明般将你旋转起来。

West Lake Dream

Midnight, gods berate a white foal in the east.
A tea leaf parachutes, tinting the flesh of this cup.
Holding their boots, men ride this planet and tell lies.
From a height, West Lake seems like a grain of white dust.

Splendid place: if only someone empties out the dust and expands it,
pouring back the greenery of dreams.
                                                                At West Lake, traces
of logic walks out of the scenery like small change lost and found.
                                                                This isn't real.

Residents in your city surround you
like around a hot pot meal. A carp leaps.
Add some vinegar for yourself. In the wind an official
slaps someone soundly in the face.
                                                          This isn't real, either—

if a teardrop vomits up a pile of fish bones.
Nickels of tears spent, and beyond tears there is a
West Lake, like *the* West Lake, brimming with hot tears,
swirling around you like dawn.

云（组诗）

1

当我，头颅盛满蔚蓝的蘑菇，
瞭望着善的行程，儿子，别说
云里有个父亲，云朵的几只梨儿
摆在碗中，这静物的某一日。

我牵看你的手，把扛着梯子的
量杯伸出窗中，接住“喂”这个词。
这是中午，或者说，
这是虚空，谁也拿它没法。

这是你的生日；祈祷在碗边
叠了只小船。我站在这儿，
而那俄底修斯还漂在海上。
在你身上，我继续等着我。

Clouds [a lyric sequence]

1

When my skull overflows with sky-blue mushrooms
watch the voyage of goodness from afar, son, don't say
there is a father in the clouds. Pears in the clouds
lay inside a bowl, this day's still life.

I tug and watch your hand, stretch out the window
a measuring cup that carries the ladder, catching the word *Hey*.
This is afternoon, or rather,
this is a void no one can do anything about.

This is your birthday; prayers by the bowl
fold a boat. I stand here
while Odysseus floats on the sea.
On your body, I continue to wait for me.

2

一片叶。这宇宙的舌头伸进
窗口，引来街尾的一片森林。
德国的晴天，罗可可的拱门，
你燕子似的元音贯穿它们。

你只要说出树，树就会
闪现在对面，无论你坐在哪儿。
但树会憋住满腔的绿意，
如果谁一边站起，一边说，

“多，就是少？未必如此。
我喜欢不多不少。”口吻慵倦。
这时，蝉的锁攫住婉鸣的浓荫，
如止痛片，淡忘之月悬在白昼。

2

A leaf. This universe stretches its tongue into
the window, luring a forest from the street's end.
Fine days in Germany, Rococo arches,
your swallow-like vowels penetrate.

When you say *tree*, a tree flashes
before your eyes no matter where you sit,
but the tree will contain its greenery,
should one stand up and say,

Is more less? Not necessarily.
I like no more, no less. A weary tone.
At that instant, the lock of cicadas clutches the singing foliage
like a painkiller. The moon of fading memory hangs in daylight.

3

这儿是哪？这是千里之外。
离哪儿最近？很难说——
也许，离远方。咫尺之外，
远方是不是一盒午餐肉罐头，

打开嚷乌托邦？远方是
旋涡的标本，有着筋骨的僻静，
也有点儿讥诮，因为太远。
所以得迷上那随意的警觉，

坐在这摇椅眺望。远方是
工具箱，被客人搁在台阶上，
一朵云演出那遇刺的哑暴君
脸“啊”地一声走漏了表情。

3

Where is here? Thousands of miles away.
Where are we nearest? Hard to say—
perhaps far away. A stone's throw away,
is *far away* a box of luncheon meat

opening to blurt out Utopia? Far away
is a sample of eddies, the seclusion of muscles and bones,
perhaps a bit cynical because it's too far,
hence the craze for random vigilance,

surveying from this rocking chair. Far away is
a toolbox, left by a guest on the steps.
A cloud plays a mute assassinated tyrant
leaking out an expression with the cry of *Ah*.

4

今天你两岁；美人鱼凭空跃起，
天上掌声一片。而摩托颤袅，
拐进世纪末。把骑的幻象怪兽般
刹到迷迭香前，你，小伙子

翻身而下，表情冷落。云呀
遍地找着鞋子，弄堂晾满西风。
百舌鸟换气，再唱：“当你
把钥匙反锁在家里，你也

反锁了雨外看雨的你。”你，
绕着落地玻璃往室内张望：
钥匙摇摇欲坠。你喊你的名字，
并看见自己朝自己走出来……

4

You turn two today; mermaids leap from thin air,
the sky applauds. A trembling motorcycle
into the turn of the century. Ride it like an illusory beast
to the front of the rosemary. You, young man,

roll down over with a neglected look. O clouds
searching everywhere for shoes, the westerly wind hangs in the lane.
Mockingbirds take in a breath and sing again, *When you*
lock the key at home, you are also locked inside,

watching rain fall beyond rain. You walk around
a fallen windowpane, peer into the room:
a key is about to drop from a keyhole. You shout
your name, watching yourself walk toward yourself . . .

5

……幻景飘逝。桌面，精灵的遗址。
上面留了颗香橙糖，自虐的
甜蜜。瞧，窗外，地球在动呢。
地心下脚手架上，人有个替身——

那儿，那背上刺着“不”的人，
饕餮昏黑的引力，嘴角
流淌着事件：明天的播音员。
云的双乳称着空想的重量，

当揉皱的一团纸，跪对着
花瓶的傲慢。诗歌看着它们
胡闹了好几天，便一走了之。
风的织布机，织着四周。

5

. . . illusions fade. The ruins of elves on a desktop.
Orange candy left on top, the sweetness
of self-mutilation. Look, the earth is moving outside the window.
On a scaffold at the earth's center, everyone has a stand-in—

a man tattooed with *No* on his back,
the gluttonous dark gravity, events running
from the corner of the mouth: tomorrow's broadcaster.
Cloud breasts weighed down with fantasy

as a crumpled ball of paper kneels before
the arrogance of a vase. Poetry watches them
screw around for days and then walk away.
The wind's loom weaves all around.

6

地平线上，护士们忙乱着。
瞧，我那祖父。他正弯腰
采草药。乌云把口袋翻出来，
红豆，在离地三尺高的祖国

时日般泻下，吸住我父亲，
使他右手脱臼，那天他比你
还小，望着高出他的我在
生气。于是，他要当书法家

尊严从云缝泄出金黄的暗语。
地平线上，护士们在撒手：
天上担架飘呀飘。你祖父般
长大。你，妙手回春者啊！

6

Nurses are bustling over the horizon.
Look, my grandfather. He's stooping
to collect herbs. Dark clouds turn out his pockets,
red beans fall like years onto the motherland

from three feet high, gluing my father,
dislocating his right hand. He is smaller
than you, angry with me who stands taller
than him. So he wants to be a calligrapher.

Dignity leaks out golden jargon from the clouds.
Nurses let go over the horizon:
stretchers drift in the sky. You grow up like a grandfather.
Your magical hands bring the dead back to life!

7

你拾起小老虎，当现实的
老虎跳跃，叨来满眼的圆满。
那是雷电。说，雷电，是它叫
苹果林中惊叹号猿人般蹦窜；

当撕毁了的东西升空，聚成
乌云之魂，浇淋遍地的图案，
未知的老虎跳跃，叨来野外；
薄荷味儿派出几个邮递员。

当母蛾背着异乡陷落杯底，
孩子，活着就是去大闹一场。
空间的老虎跳跃，飞翔，
使你午睡溢出无边的宁静。

7

You pick up a tiger cub, and like reality
the tiger leaps, a perfect prey in its mouth.
That is thunder and lightning. Say thunder, say lightning:
it makes exclamation marks leap like apes in apple groves.

When things torn apart rise into the air, coalescing
into cloud ghosts, watering visual patterns everywhere,
an unknown tiger leaps, wilderness in its mouth;
a scent of mint dispatches a postman or two.

A mother moth carries its own exile, falls to the bottom
of a cup. Child, life is about creating havoc.
Tigers leap and soar in space,
an immense tranquility spills out from your nap.

8

今天你两岁；你醒来时，
雷雨已耗尽了我心中的云朵。
下午一道回光伫立，问：
“你是谁？”而没有哪种回答

不会留个影子。这是诗艺。
影子叠着影子使黑暗蠕动起来。
尘埃，银河般聚成一股力，
寄身于这光柱，奔腾又攀谈：

“别惹我。自强不息，我
象征着什么。”只因它不可见，
瞳孔深处才溅出无穷无尽的蓝，
那种让消逝者鞠躬的蓝。

1996 Zhang Deng zu seinem zweiten Geburtstag

8

You turn two today; when you wake,
a thunderstorm will have exhausted the clouds in my heart.
A ray of afternoon light is reflected. It stands upright
for a long time and asks, *Who are you?* No response—

a shadow lingers. This is the art of poetry.
Shadows overlap and make the darkness squirm.
Dust, a force clustering like the Milky Way,
home to this beam of light. It gallops in small talk—

Don't bother me. Always strive for improvement. What
do I symbolize—and because it can't be seen,
a swash of boundless blue flows from somewhere deep
in the pupils: a blue to which the dead bow.

1996, to Zhang Deng for his second birthday

悠悠

顶楼，语音室。
秋天哐的一声来临，
清辉给四壁换上宇宙的新玻璃，
大伙儿戴好耳机，表情团结如玉。

怀孕的女老师也在听。迷离声音的
吉光片羽：
“晚报，晚报”，磁带绕地球呼啸快进。
紧张的单词，不肯逝去，如街景和
喷泉，如几个天外客站定在某边缘，
拨弄着夕照，他们猛地泻下一匹锦绣：
虚空少于一朵花！
她看了看四周的

新格局，每个人嘴里都有一台织布机，
正喃喃讲述同一个
好的故事。
每个人都沉浸在倾听中，
每个人都裸着器官，工作着，

全不察觉。

1997

Long, Long Ago

In the attic, a language lab.
Autumn comes in with a clang,
its luster replaces new glass panes of the cosmos for four walls.
We put on headphones, an expression as unified as jade.

The pregnant teacher listens too. An enchanting voice
with the remains of a precious cultural relic:
Evening Post, Evening Post. The tape howls and fast-forwards around
the world.
Nervous words refuse to fade, like street scenes and
fountains, like aliens who stand on the edge,
flirt with dusklight, unleash a skein of silk:
emptiness is less than a flower!
She looks around:

new patterns, a loom in each mouth,
uttering the same
good story.
Everyone is steeped in listening.
Everyone working away with naked organs—

totally unaware.

1997

春秋来信

1

这个时辰的背面，才是我的家，
它在另一个城市里挂起了白旗。
天还没亮，睡眠的闸门放出几辆
载重卡车，它们恐龙般在拐口
撕抢某件东西，本就没有的东西。
我醒来。
　　　　身上一颗绿扣子滚落。

2

我们的绿扣子，永恒的小赘物。

云朵，砌建着上海。
　　　　　　　　　　我心中一幅蓝图
正等着增砖添瓦。我挪向亮处，
那儿，鹤，闪现了一下。你的信
立在室中央一柱阳光中理着羽毛——
是的，无需特赦。得从小白菜里，
从豌豆苗和冬瓜，找出那一个理解来，

来关掉肥胖和机器——
　　　　　　　　　　　我深深地
被你身上的矛盾吸引，移到窗前。
四月如此清澈，好似烈酒的反光，
街景颤抖着组合成深奥的比例。
是的，我喊不醒现实。而你的声音
追上我的目力所及：“我，

Letters in Four Seasons

1

The obverse of this instance is my home.
It raises a white flag in another city.
Before dawn, sleep's floodgates let
loose a few trucks. Like dinosaurs clawing
around the corner for something that doesn't exist.
I wake up.
A green button tumbles from my body.

2

Our green button, a residue of eternity.

Clouds brick up Shanghai.
A blueprint in my heart
awaits more brick and tile. I move into a bright spot.
There, a crane flashes for a second. Your letters
stand preening in a column of light at the room's center—
yes, no need for amnesty. Perception must be sought
from inside bok choy, from pea shoots and winter melon.

Come, switch off obesity and machines—
Deeply
drawn to the contradictions of your body, I shift to the window.
Such a clear April, like light reflected from hard liquor.
A series of profound proportions in trembling street scenes.
Yes, my screams can't wake reality. Yet your voice
catches the limits of my sight. *I*—

就是你呀！我也漂在这个时辰里。
工地上就要爆破了，我在我这边
鸣这面锣示警。游过来呀，
接住这面锣，它就是你错过了的一切。”

3

我拾起地上的绿扣子，吹了吹。
开始忙我的事儿。
　　　　　　　　静的时候，
窗下经过的邮差以为我是我的肖像；
有时我趴在桌面昏昏欲睡，
双手伸进空间，像伸进一付镣铐，

哪儿，哪儿，是我们的精确呀？
　　　　　　　　　　　　　　……绿扣子。

1997 赠臧棣

am you! I'm also drifting in this hour.
The construction site is about to explode. I'm right here
striking the gong to raise the alarm. Swim over here!
Catch this gong, it's everything you've missed.

3

I pick up the green button from the floor and blow on it.
Busy myself with life.
                                        In the stillness,
a postman passing by the window thinks I'm my own portrait—
sometimes I sprawl across the table drowsily,
hands reaching into emptiness, like reaching into a pair of handcuffs.

Where, where is our precision?
                                                    . . . Green button.

1997, for Zang Di

瞧，弟弟，这些空瓶子……

迈阿密——我俩都不在那里，
但一瓶XO酒
却叫我俩在景点中晃荡。那里，
棕榈树的肌肉隆起。你，挣脱了五花大绑，
舔着流到手腕背的冰淇淋，破涕而笑。
古怪的句法，骑着出租车内冷气的忧郁
勾幻出一股令人下坠的异香："每天，
天上像是有一个篮球场似的。"我想象你
飞跃，投篮。"但囚禁我的空间，
却越缩越小，最后小得不比一个硬币大。"
你比划着，仿佛脏，咸，铁窗和
刷得墨绿的墙，就潜伏在人体的关节里。

电，就那么一点点；到处都漏电。蝴蝶
管制那么几瓦电，抖簌在标语上。"每天，
我梦见甜，可口可乐的那种甜。"
闷雷
响着，大海冒青烟，龙卷风竖起它的
迷光的廊柱，那里，摩天楼如鹿群的蹄惊跑，

那里，我醉卧在空空的篮球场，梦见
监狱碎了，你醒在一个管理员似的且比未来
更耐久的，空瓶子边，对着现实发呆。

1996

Look, Brother, These Empty Bottles . . .

Miami—neither of us was there,
                                        but a bottle of XO whisky
made us sway in its scenery. There,
muscles of palm trees bulged. Trussed up, you broke free, licked
the ice cream dripping down to your wrists and burst from tears into laughter.
Odd syntax rode on the melancholia of an air-conditioned taxi
and outlined a drooping, peculiar fragrance: *Every day*
the sky seems to contain a basketball court. I imagined you
leaping to give it a shot. *But the space that imprisons me*
shrinks until it is no bigger than a coin.
You pantomimed as if dirt, salt, iron windows, and
walls scrubbed into dark green were lurking in a human's joints.

Electricity, scant; leakage everywhere. Butterflies
controlled the few watts of current, quivering on a slogan. *Every day*
I dream of sweetness, the sweetness of Coca Cola.
                                                            Dull thunder
roared, green smoke billowed from the sea, a tornado straightened its
column of dazzling light. There, skyscrapers stampeded like the deer hooves;

there, I lay drunk on an empty basketball court, dreaming
of the shattered prison. And you woke up next to an empty bottle—its
supervision more lasting than the future—staring blankly at reality.

1996

边缘

像只西红柿躲在秤的边上，他总是
躺着。有什么闪过，警告或燕子，但他
一动不动，守在小东西的旁边。秒针移到
十点整，闹钟便邈然离去了；一支烟
也走了，携着几副变了形的蓝色手拷。
他的眼镜，云，德国锁。总之，没走的
都走了。
　　　　空，变大。他隔得更远，但总在
某个边缘：齿轮的边上，水的边上，他自个儿的
边上。他时不时望着天，食指向上，
练着细瘦而谵狂的书法："回来"！
果真，那些走了样的都又返回了原样：
新区的窗满是晚风，月亮酿着一大桶金啤酒；
秤，猛地倾斜，那儿，无限，
像一头息怒的狮子
卧到这只西红柿的身边。

1996

Edge

Like a tomato hidden on the edge of a scale, he's always
lying flat. A flash—a warning or a swallow—he
remains still, guarding a small object. The second hand moves
to ten o'clock sharp, the alarm clock fades; a cigarette
leaves with several deformed blue handcuffs.
His spectacles, clouds, a German lock. In short, what wasn't gone
is gone.
Emptiness grows. Set apart but always somewhere
on the edge: on the edge of a gearwheel, on the edge of water and his own
self. From time to time he gazes at the sky, points his index finger,
and practices fine but delirious calligraphy: *Come back!*
Indeed, those out of shape now return to form:
evening breezes through new district's windows, the moon brews a barrel
of golden ale;
the balance suddenly tilts, there—an infinity
like an appeased lion
lying beside this tomato.

1996

大地之歌

1

逆着鹤的方向飞，当十几架美军隐形轰炸机
　偷偷潜回赤道上的母舰，有人

心如暮鼓。
　　　　　而你呢，你枯坐在这片林子里想了
　一整天，你要试试心的浩渺到底有无极限。
你边想边把手伸进内裤，当一声细软的口音说：
　“如果没有耐心，侬就会失去上海”。
你在这一万多公里外想着它电信局的中心机房，
　和落在瓷砖地上的几颗话梅核儿。
　　　　　　　　　　　　　　那些
通宵达旦的东西，刹不住的东西；一滴饮水
和它不肯屈服于化合物的上亿个细菌。
你越想就越焦虑，因为你不能禁止你爱人的
　咏叹调这天果真脱颖而出，谢幕后很干渴，
那些有助于破除窒息的东西；那些空洞如蓝图
　又使邻居围拢一瓶酒的东西；那些曲曲折折
　但最终是好的东西；使秤翘向斤斤计较又
　忠实于盈满的东西；使地铁准时发自真实并
　让忧郁症免费乘坐三周的东西；
那会是什么呢？
诱人如一盘韭黄炒鳝丝：那是否就是大地之歌？

Earth Song

1

Against the flight of cranes, when ten or more American stealth bombers
secretly dive back to the depot ship at the equator, a

heart strikes like sunset drums.
And you, sitting idly in these woods, pondering
the whole day, you test the infinity of a heart's expanse.
Pondering, you slip your hand into underwear. A voice in a delicate accent says,
Without patience, you will lose Shanghai.
Beyond ten thousand kilometers you think of its generator room at the
central telecom,
and fallen plum pits on the ceramic tile floor.
Those
overnight stuff, unstoppable; a drop of drinking water
and its hundred million germs refusing to stoop to chemical compounds.
The more you ponder the more you worry: you can't forbid your lover's
aria from standing out, parched after the curtain call.
Things that help to cure asphyxia; things as empty as a blueprint
yet bringing neighbors together over a bottle of wine; things that meander
but eventually work; things that tilt the balance to a calculating mind yet
faithfully filled to the brim; things that allow subways to run
timely and authentically
and let depression enjoy three weeks of free rides;
what could that be?
Alluring as a dish of fried chives and shredded eel, could it be the earth's song?

2

人是戏剧，人不是单个。
有什么总在穿插，联结，总想戳破空虚，并且
　仿佛在人之外，渺不可见，像
　　　　　　　　　　　　　　　　　　　　　鹤……

3

你不是马勒，但马勒有一次也捂着胃疼，守在
　角落。你不是马勒，却生活在他虚拟的未来之中，
　迷离地忍着，
马勒说：这儿用五声音阶是合理的，关键得加弱音器，
　关键是得让它听上去就像来自某个未知界的
　微弱的序曲。错，不要紧，因为完美也会含带
　另一个问题，
一位女伯爵翘起小拇指说它太长，
　马勒说：不，不长。

4

此刻早已是未来。
　　　　　　　　　　　　　　　但有些人总是迟了七个小时，
他们对大提琴与晾满弄堂衣裳的呼应
　竟一无所知。

那些生活在凌乱皮肤里的人；
　　　　　　　　　　　　　　　　　　　　摩天楼里
那些猫着腰修一台传真机，以为只是哪个小部件
　出了毛病的人，（他们看不见那故障之鹤，正
　屏息敛气，口衔一页图解，踱立在周围）；
那些偷税漏税还向他们的小女儿炫耀的人；
那些因搞不到假公章而煽自己耳光的人；

2

People are dramas, people are not singular.
Something alternates, connects, in hopes of puncturing the void,
as if beyond people, invisibly small, like
cranes . . .

3

You aren't Mahler, but Mahler once hid his stomachache, muffled
in a corner. You aren't Mahler but are living in his virtual future,
enduring in a haze.
Mahler says, *It makes sense to use a pentatonic scale here. The key is to add a sordine,*
to make it sound like a frail prelude from a terra
incognita. Mistakes are alright, for perfection comes with
another problem.
A countess tilts her pinkie and says it's too long.
No, says Mahler. *Not at all.*

4

This instant, already in the future.
But those who are always seven hours late
know not an inkling of the cello and the echo of clothes hung
along the lane.

Those who live in cluttered skin;
in skyscrapers
those who bend down to repair a fax machine, thinking it's just an issue
of some component (they can't see the crane of failure, breath-
less, a page of illustration gagged, walking on tiptoe);
those who evade taxes and brag about it in front of their daughters;
those who can't obtain a fake seal and slap themselves;

那些从不看足球赛又蔑视接吻的人；
那些把诗写得跟报纸一模一样的人，并咬定
　那才是真实，咬定讽刺就是讽刺别人
　而不是抓自己开心，因而抱紧一种倾斜，
　几张嘴凑到一起就说同行坏话的人；
那些决不相信三只茶壶没装水也盛着空之饱满的人，
　也看不出室内的空间不管如何摆设也
　去不掉一个隐藏着的蠕动的疑问号；
那些从不赞美的人，从不宽宏的人，从不发难的人；
那些对云朵模特儿的扭伤漠不关心的人；
那些一辈子没说过也没喊过“特赦”这个词的人；
那些否认对话是为孩子和环境种植绿树的人；

他们同样都不相信：这只笛子，这只给全城血库
　供电的笛子，它就是未来的关键。
　一切都得仰仗它。

5

鹤之眼：里面储存了多少张有待冲洗的底片啊！

6

如何重建我们的大上海，这是一个大难题：

首先，我们得仰仗一个幻觉，使我们能盯着
　某个深奥细看而不致晕眩，并看见一片叶
　（铃鼓伴奏了一会儿），它的脉络
　呈现出最优化的公路网，四通八达；
我们得相信一瓶牛奶送上门就是一瓶牛奶而不是
　别的；

those who never watch soccer yet disdain kissing;
those who write poetry like newsprint, insisting
    on the truth, insisting that satire is to lampoon others
    and not self-deprecate, hence adhering to a slant;
    those who speak ill of peers when they gather;
those who never believe that three teapots without water are also full
                        of emptiness,
    or can't tell the emptiness of an interior regardless of its decoration
    can't be rid of a hidden wriggling question mark;
those who never praise, never act magnanimous, never attack others;
those who do not care for the clouds and models and their sprains;
those who have never once in their life pronounced the word *amnesty*;
those who deny dialogue as a way to plant trees for their children and
                        the environment;

likewise they don't believe: this flute, which supplies power for blood banks
    for the entire city is the key to the future.
    Everything relies on it.

5

Eyes of a crane: many negatives waiting to be developed are stored inside!

6

Rebuilding our Shanghai is a huge challenge:

first, we must rely on an illusion, which lets us stare close
    at profundity without feeling giddy and see a leaf
    (brief tambourine accompaniment), its skeleton
    presenting the most optimal road network in every direction;
we must believe that a bottle of home-delivered milk is a bottle of milk and not
    anything else;

我们得有一个电话号码，能遏止哭泣；
我们得有一个派出所，去领回我们被反绑的自己；
我们得学会笑，当一大一小两只西红柿上街玩，
大的对小的说："Catch-up!"；

我们得发誓不偷书，不穿鳄鱼皮鞋，不买可乐；
我们得发明宽敞，双面的清洁和多向度的
　透明，一如鹤的内心；

是呀，我们得仰仗每一台吊车，它恐龙般的
　骨节爱我们而不会让我们的害怕像
　失手的号音那样滑溜在头皮之上；
如果一班人开会学文件，戒备森严，门窗紧闭，
　我们得知道他们究竟说了我们什么；
我们得有一个"不"的按钮，装在伞把上；
我们得有一部好法典，像
　田纳西的山顶上有一只瓮；
而这一切，
这一切，正如马勒说的，还远远不够，

还不足以保证南京路不迸出轨道，不足以阻止
　我们看着看着电扇旋闪一下子忘了
　自己的姓名，坐着呆想了好几秒，比
　文明还长的好几秒，直到中午和街景，隔壁
　保姆的安徽口音，放大的米粒，洁水器，
　小学生的广播操，刹车，蝴蝶，突然
　归还原位：一切都似乎既在这儿，
　　　　　　　　　　　　　　　　又在
飞啊。
鹤，
不只是这与那，而是
一切跟一切都相关；

we must have a phone number to curb weeping;
we must have a local police station to claim back the selves with bound hands;
we must learn to smile when two tomatoes, big and small, play on the street,
and to the small tomato the bigger one says, *Catch up!*

we must swear not to steal books, wear leather crocodile shoes, or buy Coke;
we must invent spaciousness, a two-sided cleanliness and multidimensional
    transparency, like the inner world of a crane;

yes, we must rely on every hoist, its dinosauric
    joints love us but do not let our fear
    slide on scalps like goofy bugle calls;
if a group of men meet to learn software, strictly guarded, doors and
                                        windows shut,
    we must know precisely what they say about us;
we must have a *No* button fixed to an umbrella handle;
we must have a good code like
    an urn at the Appalachian summit
while all of this,
all this, as Mahler says, is far from enough,

far from ensuring Nanjing Road from going off the rails, far from stopping
    us to watch as an electric fan spins and we forget
    our own names, sitting and mooning for seconds, seconds longer
    than civilization, until midday and street scenes, a next-door
    nanny and her Anhui accent, a magnified rice grain, water filter,
    radio calisthenics for elementary students, brakes, butterflies, suddenly
    back to their original place: all seems here,
                                                                        and

flying.
Crane,
not just here and there but
everything has something to do with everything;

三度音程摆动的音型。双簧管执拗地导入新动机。
马勒又说，是的，黄浦公园也是一种真实，
　但没有幻觉的对位法我们就不能把握它。
我们得坚持在它正对着
　浦东电视塔的景点上，为你爱人塑一座雕像：
　她失去的左乳，用一只闹钟来接替，她
　骄傲而高耸，洋溢着补天的意态。
指针永远下岗在12:21，
　这沸腾的一秒，她低回咏叹：我
满怀渴望，因为人映照着人，没有陌生人；
人人都用手拨动着地球；
这一秒，
　　　　至少这一秒，我每天都有一次坚守了正确
　并且警示：
　　　　　　仍有一种至高无上……

1999 赠东东

musical motifs swayed by minor thirds. Stubborn oboes import a new motif.
Mahler adds, *Yes, Huangpu Park is also a reality,*
    but without illusory counterpoint we cannot grasp it.
We must stand by the scenic spot
    of the Oriental Pearl Tower en face, build a statue for your lover:
    her lost left breast replaced by an alarm clock, she
    soars with pride, steeped in the pose of patching the sky.
The pointer always gets off work at 12:21,
    at this bubbling second she lets out a low deep aria, *I*
brim with eagerness, for each casts light upon the other and there's no stranger;
everyone prods the globe with their hands;
in this second,
                at least this instant, I would stick to being correct once a day
    and caution,
                A supremacy yet reigns . . .

1999, for Dongdong

到江南去

我们相隔万里正谈着虎骨，肥皂剧，樟树
和琴，忽然电话“嘎”地一串响，像是
卫星掉落了：漆黑。你丢失在你正在的地方。
话筒里仿佛憋着监听者带酒气的屏息，
和哗啦啦的翻纸声，若有若无的浑沌，或
大水，它正乌云滚滚地倒映在碎玻璃之上；
窗：有个胖姨在朝天喊谁下来搬煤气罐。
你会在哪儿呢，这一瞬，是否荒蛮果真
重临？
　　　你，奥尔弗斯主义者，你还会
返回吗？线路，这冷却的走廊，仍通着，
我不禁迎了上去：对，到江南去！我看见
那尽头外亮出十里荷花，南风折叠，它
像一个道理，在阡陌上蹦着，向前扑着，
又变成一件鼓满的、没有脑袋的白背心，
时而被绊在野渡边的一个发廊外，时而
急走，时而狂暴地抱住那奔进城的火车头，
寻找幸福，用虚无的四肢。
　　　　　　　　　　　对，到江南去！
解开人身上多年来的死结：比如，对一碗
藕粉之甜不恰切的态度，对某个细节的争议，
对一个篮球场的曲解：它就在报社的对面，
那儿，夕照铺了成吨厚的红地毯，它多想
善待你啊；那儿，你忘了你的白背心和
眼镜：大地的篮球场，比天堂更陌生！

1999，赠钟鸣，liebem Freund der vielen Fernen

Off to Jiangnan

Miles apart we discuss tiger bones, soap operas, camphor trees
and *qin* music. Suddenly the phone lets out a string of screeching *ga*, like
a falling satellite: pitch-dark. You are lost exactly where you are.
The phone seems muffled by the listener's alcohol breath,
and the noisy shuffling of paper turned, the faintly discernible chaos, or
grand water reflected upon shattered glass as rolling dark clouds;
a window: a fat lady yells for someone to move the gas tank.
Where will you be, at this instant, will the wasteland really
return?
                    You, an Orphist, will you still
return? The line, this cooling corridor, still works,
I can't help but hail: *Yes, off to Jiangnan!* I can see
miles of lotuses emerging from beyond, the south wind folded,
like a reason leaping on crisscrossing paths, rushing forward,
then turning into a bloated and brainless white singlet,
sometimes tripped outside the hair salon by a bleak ferry, sometimes
hurrying past, sometimes violently clinging to the locomotive that rushes
                                        into the city,
seeking happiness, using four limbs of nothingness.
                                                                        Yes, off to Jiangnan!
Undo the fast knot on bodies for years: for instance, the inaccurate stance
toward the sweetness of a bowl of lotus root powder, disputes over a detail,
distortions of a basketball court: opposite the newspaper bureau,
there, sunset has paved a red carpet tons deep, how it longs
to be kind to you; there, you've forgotten your white singlet and
eyeglasses: the basketball court of the universe, stranger than heaven!

1999, for Zhong Ming, my dear friend far away

世界

这个世界里还呈现另一个世界，
一个跟这个世界一模一样的
世界——不不，不是另一个而是
同一个。是一个同时也是两个

世界。
　　　　因而我信赖那看不见的一切。
夜已深，我坐在封闭的机场，
往你没有的杯中
倾倒烈酒。
　　　　　　　没有的燕子的脸。
正因为你戴着别人的
戒指，
我们才得以如此亲近。

World

Another world emerges in this world.
A world just like this
world—no, no, not another but
the same. One and two

worlds.
              This is why I trust what remains invisible.
Late at night, I sit at the closed airport,
pouring hard liquor into
your empty glass.
                              No swallow's face.
Because you're wearing someone else's
ring,
we become intimate.

钻墙者和极端的倾听之歌

钻机的狂飚，启动新世纪的冲锋姿态，
在墙的另一边：
　　　　　　　　　　　　　　呜，嗷，呜嗷！
阵痛横溢桌面，退闪，直到它的细胞
被瓦解，被洞穿，被逼迫聚成窗外
浮云般的涣散的暗淡。你试图确定
钻点在何处。在墙的右上额，不，在
左边偏中的某一点上。不，整个墙
在哆嗦迸裂，追踪的目光如两只蝙蝠
撞落到地面。
　　　　　　　　　　　钻墙者半跪着，头戴
安全帽。他钻入的那个确实的一点
变成墙的另一面的
猜疑，残碎，绝望，和
凌乱的腥风。工具箱在膝盖边，
　　敞开着：
这些筋骨，意志，喧旋的欲望，使每个
方向都逆转成某个前方。
机油的芬芳仿佛前方有个贝多芬。
钻墙者半跪着，眼神绷紧——
莫非前方果真会有一个中心？
因而即使前方像镜子，
也得置身其中？
他爱前方那肉感的羁绊。
他爱前方那含金的预言。
他爱虚随着工具箱的那只黄鹂鸟，
伶俐而三维的活泼，
颤鸣婉啼，似乎仍有一个真实的外景，
有一角未经剪贴的现实，他爱

Song of a Wall Driller and the Ultimate Ear

The wild gale of a drill triggers the charge of the new century
on the other side of the wall.
Woo, ao, woo-ao!
Pangs of pain overflow the table, dodge and retreat, until its cells
dissolve, pierced through, forced to gel into a slack gray
drifting like clouds beyond the window. You try to pinpoint
the drilled hole. On the wall's upper right forehead, no, on
a certain point closer to the left of center. No, the whole wall
trembles and bursts, gazes tracking it like two bats
striking the ground.
The wall driller kneels halfway, wearing
a safety helmet. The dot he has drilled
becomes on the other side of the wall
suspicion, broken pieces, despair, and
a chaotic, foul wind. Toolbox at the knees,
wide open:
these muscles and bones, willpower, the noisy rotating desire, reversing
in every direction the way ahead.
Beethoven seems to lie ahead of the fragrance of motor oil.
The wall driller kneels halfway, looking tense—
could it indeed be a center ahead?
So even if what lay ahead resembled a mirror,
must one stay in the picture?
He loves the sensual fetters ahead.
He loves the prophecy with gold ahead.
He loves following the toolbox's yellow oriole at a distance,
its liveliness bright and three-dimensional,
graceful churring, as if an authentic outdoor setting still existed,
a corner reality yet to be cut and pasted. He loves

钻头逼完逆境之逆的那一瞬突然
陷入的虚幻，慌乱的余力，
　　踏空的马蹄，在
墙的另一面，那阴影摆设的峭壁上。
　　　　　　　　　　　　　　　　　你
预感到一种来临，虽然你不能确定那
突破点，在这边墙上，你的内部。
是的——
浩茫袭上心头。闭上眼。让它进来，
带着它的心脏，
　　一切异质的悖反的跳荡。
消化它。爱它。爱你恨的。
　　一切化合的，
错的。腾空你的内部，搬迁同时代的
家具，设想这间房
　在任何异地而因地制宜。
呜，嗷，呜嗷！
　　　　　　　　　喧嚣的粒子激荡，眼前
腾起一幅古战争的图景，
　镶入一个凭虚而
变形的，袅动的框架，逸散着，
　漂移着，使
室内谛听的空间外延，唉，这么多
男人必须嘶喊和倒毙，这么多马匹
只剩下身体的一小半，这么多鹰鹫和
历史的闪失：
　这就是每克噪音内蕴的真谛。
“是你，既发明喧嚣，又骑着喧嚣来
救我？表象凹凸，零散，冷。”呜嗷！
突然，静寂——
　　　　　　　　　闹粒子中断，落下。

the sudden instant of sinking into illusion when the drill
forces through the most adverse of adversity, the remaining strength
for fluster,
hooves kicking in the air, on
the other side of the wall, on the cliff furnished by shadows.
You
anticipate an arrival, though you can't confirm that
breakpoint, your interior stays on this side of the wall.
Yes—
you feel an onrush of vastness. Close your eyes, let it enter
with its heart,
the heterogenous and contradictory pulse of everything.
Digest it. Love it. Love what you hate.
Everything digestible
and wrong. Empty out your interior, move furniture
of the same era, imagine this room
tailored for any foreign land.
Woo, ao, woo-ao!
Grains of din agitate before your eyes
rousing the scene of an old battle,
fitting into a hollow,
metamorphic, moving frame, vaporized,
wandering,
the attentive and listening inner space extends, sigh, so many
men must yell and drop dead, so many horses
left with half-bodies, so many eagles and vultures and
mishaps of history:
this is the intrinsic meaning of each voice.
Are you the one who invented clamor yet ride on clamor
to save me? A bumpy presentation, scattered, cold. Woo-ao!
Suddenly silence—
raucous particles halt, fall.

喂，兄弟，我
在这儿。在尘埃的中心。
菊花在桌上。
一杯水，如仪典，握在你掌心。
你的那边，秋阳泻下一段锦绣，
换下窗帘。
工具箱边的那只黄鹂鸟
跃到你肩头。
水清澈无比，犹如第一次映照人像。
我听见你在咬苹果。
甜的细珠喷礴，又
缤纷地祝福般落下。喂，兄弟：
一切都会落入静寂中，不，
落入空白中，像此刻。难道不是吗？
喂！水晃了晃。空白圆满，大而无外。
其内核有饱实之磁
归纳一切喧嚣，项目和头发：落下，
　回归——
还原成窗外临风咏望的苹果林。
喂，mon semblable，我看不见你的脸，
但我
仿佛听见了你的表情，
　那是休息的表情，
红润的，好的。
清澈是空白的手套，
摆弄事物的方式。
我听见你的自语
分叉成对白，像在跟谁争辩。
　而墙，只是
一个布景，
　一个不能成为其实物的称谓。
你钻找的中心，没有。我们必须团结。

Hi, brother, I
am here. At the center of the dust.
Chrysanthemums on the table.
A glass of water, like a ceremony, in your grip.
On your side, brocade pours from the autumn sun,
curtains change.
The golden oriole by the toolbox
leaps onto your shoulder.
Water clear beyond comparison, as if casting light on a portrait.
I hear you bite an apple.
Fine beards of sweetness in an upsurge, then
fall in a riot of colors like blessings. Hi, brother:
everything will fall into silence, no,
into emptiness, like this instant. *N'est-ce pas?*
Hi! Water sways. A perfect emptiness, huge but without an exterior.
Its kernel contains the magnetism of true vigor,
which sums up the commotion, a project, and hair: fall,
    return—
reduced to charming apple wood that sings with the wind, gazes afar
                                        outside the window.
Hi, *mon semblable,* I can't see your face,
but I
seem to hear your expression,
    the expression of rest,
Rosy and nice.
Clear are the empty gloves,
the way to move things around.
I hear you mutter,
fork into a dialogue like in a dispute with someone.
    But the wall is just
a decor,
    a prefix that can't materialize as a wall.
The center you drill and look for does not exist. We must unite.

我拍打我的墙告诉你。
　我听见你在听。
你关掉你衣裳兜里的小收音机，
贝多芬的提琴曲嘎然而止，
如梯子被抽走。
我听见你换钻头，
　　　　　　　　它失手坠地，而空白
激昂地回荡而四溅！
我听见你换好了钻头，而危机
半含机遇，负面多神奇，我，几乎是你
——
呜，嗷，呜嗷！空白的
钻机放歌：
　　　　　喧嚣只是静寂的工装裤，
一切合一又含众多，
　空白依托的形形色色，
以致我们被允许
望出窗口并且朗读：
苹果林就在外面，外面的里面，
苹果林确实在那儿，
源自空白，附丽于空白，
　　　　　　　　　　信赖它……

I tell you by beating the wall.
    I can hear you listening.
You switch off the portable radio in your pocket,
Beethoven's violin screeches to a halt
like a ladder pulled away.
I hear you change a drill,
                        it falls with a slip, while emptiness
reverberates excitedly before it splatters.
I hear you fix a new drill, while a crisis
holds a partial opportunity, how magical the cons, I am almost you
——

Woo, ao, woo-ao! The empty
drill sings aloud,
                Clamor the cargo pants for stillness,
everything as one yet of multitude,
        emptiness relies on diversity,
which allows us
to look out the window and recite,
Apple woods are outside, the inside of outside,
apple woods are there,
from emptiness, connected to emptiness,
                                trust them . . .

醉时歌

昨夜，当晚会向左袅袅漂移，酒
突然甜得鞠躬起来。音符的活虾儿
从大提琴蹦遛出来，又“唰”地
立正在酒妙处，仿佛欢迎谁去革命，
有个胖子边哭边从西装内兜掏出一挂鞭炮，
但没有谁理他。唉，不要近得这么远，
七八个你不要把头发甩来甩去，
茶壶里的解放区不要倾泻，绽碎，
不要对我鞠躬，鹿在桌下呦鸣，
有个干部模样的人踮足，举杯，用
零钱的口吻对外宾说：“吃鸡吧”，
酒提前笑了。我继续向左漂移，我
就是那个胖子？怎么也点不亮那挂鞭炮
我的心在万里外一间空电话亭吟唱，
是否有个刺客会如约而来？地球
露出了蓝尾巴，只有一条湿腻的毛巾
递了过来，一叶空舟自寒波间折回。
东倒西歪啊，让我们从它身上
提炼出另一个东三省，一条高速路，
通向袅娜多姿，通向七八个你，
你叫小翠，这会儿不见了，或许
正偎着石狮朝万里外那电话亭拨手机，
（她的小爱人约好来那儿等电话，
但他没来，她想象着那边的空幻）。
她回到这儿，四周正在崩溃，仿佛
对面满是风信子。一个老混混晃过来，
与谁干杯。性格从各人的手指尖
滴漏着，胖子的鞭炮还没点燃，

Drunken Song

Last night, when the banquet drifted to the left in a curl, wine
suddenly sweetened until it could bow. Notes like living shrimps
leapt and strolled from the cello, then *swish—*
they stood right up in the beauty of wine, like welcoming so-and-so for
a revolution.
A fat man cried as he fished out a string of firecrackers from his suit,
but no one cared. *Hey, don't close in from a distance,*
the seven or eight of you, don't shake your hair here and there,
don't spill and shatter the liberated zone from the teapot,
don't bow to me, a deer is bleating under the table.
Like a party official someone stood on his toes, raised his glass, and
in a petty tone told the guests to *eat chicken.*
The wine smiled in advance. I kept drifting to the left. *Am I*
that fat man? In spite of this, the string of firecrackers failed to light up.
My heart sang in an empty phone booth ten thousand miles away,
Will an assassin arrive as promised? The world
revealed its blue tail, passing on a damp and oily
towel, an empty boat turned back through cold waves.
Staggering sideways, let's refine from its body
another Manchuria, a highway
to willowy grace, to the seven or eight of you,
you, Xiaocui, vanished instantly, maybe cuddling
up against a stone lion, dialing your cell phone to a phone booth miles away
(her lover gave his word to wait there for the call,
but he didn't show up, so she imagined the illusion on the other end).
She came back, the surroundings on the brink of a downfall, as if
full of hyacinths on the opposite side. An old slacker swayed,
toasting so-and-so. Drops of character spilled from their
fingertips, the fat man's firecrackers still unlit,

有人把打火机夺了过去，“我心里，”
胖子呕吐道：“清楚得很，不，朕，”
胖子拍拍自己，“朕，心里有数。”
刺客软了下来。厅外，冰封锁着消息。
“向左，向左，”胖子把刺客扶进厕所。
刺客亲了缺席一口，像亲了亲秦王。
秦王啊缺席如刺客。而我，像那
胖子，朝遍地的天意再三鞠躬；我或是
那醉汉，万里外，碰巧在电话亭旁，
听着铃声，蹀躞过来，却落后于沉寂，
那醉汉等在那空电话亭边，唱啊唱：
“远方啊远方，你有着本地的抽象！”

but someone had snatched his lighter away. *In my heart,*
the fat man vomited, *I know very well . . . no, I,*
the fat man said and slapped himself, *I'm well aware.*
The assassin softened. Outside, news was ice-sealed.
Left, left. The fat man helped the assassin into the toilet.
The assassin kissed absence like kissing Emperor Qin.
O Emperor Qin, as absent as the assassin. But like the fat
man, I bowed three times before Heaven's will. I could be
that drunkard ten thousand miles away, who chanced by a phone booth,
heard the phone ring, paced up and down but fell behind a silence.
Waiting by an empty phone booth, the drunkard sang and sang,
Afar, O afar, you're blessed with local abstraction!

告别孤独堡

1

上午，仿佛有一种樱桃之远；有
一杯凉水在口中微微发甜，
使人竟置身到他自身之外
电话铃响了三下，又杳然中断，
会是谁呢？
我忽然记起两天前回这儿的夜路上，
我设想去电话亭给我的空房间拨电话：
假如真的我听到我在那边
对我说："Hello？"
我的惊恐，是否会一窝蜂地钻进听筒？

2

你没有来电话，而我
两小时之后又将分身异地。
秋天正把它的帽子收进山那边的箱子里。
燕子，给言路铺着电缆，仿佛

有一种羁绊最终能被俯瞰……

3

有一种怎样的渺不可见
泄露在窗台上，袖子边：
有一种抵抗之力，用打火机
对空旷派出一只狐狸，那

Adieu Schloss Solitude

1

Morning, like cherries at a distance; a
glass of cool water sweetening on the tongue,
removing one from oneself.
The phone rings three times and stops.
Who is it?
I suddenly recall my way here from two nights back,
imagine how I'd dial up my empty room from a phone booth:
if I could really hear myself on the other end
saying *Hello?*
would my panic swarm into the receiver?

2

You never phone, but I
will again find myself in a foreign land in two hours.
Autumn is keeping its hat in a chest on that mountainside.
Swallows, laying cables for communication, like

a yoke that can be looked down at last . . .

3

What form of misty invisibility
is exposed on a windowsill, by the sleeves:
a form of resistance using a lighter
to dispatch a fox into the open, those

颉颃的瞬翼
使森林边一台割草机猛省地跪向静寂，

使睡衣在衣架上鼓起胸肌，它
登上预感
如登上去市中心的班车。

4

是呀，我们约好去沙漠，它是
绿的妆镜，那儿，你会给它
带来唯一的口红，纸和卫生品；
但去那儿，我们得先等候在机场的咖啡亭。

是呀，樱桃多远。而咖啡，仿佛
知道你不会来而使过客颤抖。
咖啡推开一个纹身的幻象，空间弯曲，而
有一种对称，
命令左中指冲刺般翘起：

“决不给纳粹半点机会！”

wings that soar and blink,
make a mower by the woods kneel in sudden quiet revelation,

make pajamas on the hanger expand their pecs. It
mounts onto a premonition
like boarding a downtown shuttle bus.

4

Oh yes, we have planned to go to the desert. It is
a green makeup mirror. There, you will bring it
the one and only lipstick, napkins, sanitary products—
to go there, we must first wait at the airport coffee kiosk.

Oh yes, cherries are far off. And coffee, seemingly
aware that you won't come, makes travelers tremble.
Coffee nudges off a tattooed illusion. Space meanders, yet
a form of symmetry
summons the left middle finger to tilt in a spurt:

Never ever spare the Nazis!

父亲

1962年，他不知道该怎么办。他，
还年轻，很理想，也蛮左的，却戴着
右派的帽子。他在新疆饿得虚胖，
逃回到长沙老家。他祖母给他炖了一锅
猪肚萝卜汤，里边还漂着几粒红枣儿。
室内烧了香，香里有个向上的迷惘。
这一天，他真的是一筹莫展。
他想出门遛个弯儿，又不大想。

他盯着看不见的东西，哈哈大笑起来。
他祖母递给他一支烟，他抽了，第一次。
他说，烟圈弥散着"咄咄怪事"这几个字。
中午，他想去湘江边的橘子洲头坐一坐，
去练练笛子。
他走着走着又不想去了，
他沿着来路往回走，他突然觉得
总有两个自己，
一个顺着走，
一个反着走，
一个坐到一匹锦绣上吹歌，
而这一个，走在五一路，走在不可泯灭的
真实里。

他想，现在好了，怎么都行啊。
他停下。他转身。他又朝橘子洲头的方向走去。
他这一转身，惊动了天边的一只闹钟。
他这一转身，搞乱了人间所有的节奏。
他这一转身，一路奇妙，也

变成了我的父亲。

Father

In 1962, he had no idea what to do in life. He
was still young, idealistic, quite leftist, yet with
the repute of a rightist. In Xinjiang he starved into a puffy man,
fled back to Changsha. His grandma stewed him a pot
of pork tripe and carrot soup with floating red dates.
Incense burned in the house, rising in a maze.
That day he was at his wits' end.
He wanted to take a walk but hesitated.

He stared at the invisible and laughed out loud.
His grandma passed him a cigarette. He smoked for the first time.
He said, *A wisp of smoke traces the word* absurdity.
In the afternoon, he wanted to rest on Orange Isle
and practice his flute.
On the way he changed his mind.
He took the same route back, suddenly realizing
there were two selves—
one walking forward,
one backward,
one playing a song on a bolt of brocade,
and this one, walking along a Labor Day Street, in a lasting
truth.

He thought, *Well, anything will do.*
He stopped. He turned around. Walked back to Orange Isle.
He turned around, startling an alarm clock in the sky.
He turned around, messing up the world's rhythm.
He turned around—miracles en route—and

became my father.

枯坐

枯坐的时候，我想，那好吧，就让我

像一对夫妇那样搬到海南岛
去住吧，去住到一个新奇的节奏里——
那男的是体育老师，那女的很聪明，会炒股；
就让我住到他们一起去买锅碗瓢盆时
胯骨叮当响的那个节奏里。
在路边摊，
那女的第一次举起一个椰子，喝一种
说不出口的沁甜；那男的望着海，指了指
带来阵雨的乌云里的一个熟人模样，说：你看，
那像谁？那女的抬头望，又惊疑地看了看
他。突然，他们俩捧腹大笑起来。

那女的后来总结说：
我们每天都随便去个地方，去偷一个
惊叹号，
就这样，我们熬过了危机。

赠 Y. L.

Sitting Idly

Sitting idly, I thought: Well, just let me

move to Hainan Island like a married couple.
Go live there, live in a novel rhythm—
the man, a PE teacher; the woman, quite smart, speculates in stocks and shares.
Just let me live in the rhythm of tinkling hip bones
when they buy pots and pans together.
By a roadside stall,
the woman lifts up a coconut for the first time, drinks an
inexplicable, oozing sweetness; the man gazes at the sea, points
at what seems like an acquaintance in a black cloud bringing a shower,
                    and says, *Look,*
who does he look like? The woman looks up and glances at him,
bewildered. Suddenly, both of them burst into laughter.

Later, she concludes:
Every day we visit a random place, steal
an exclamation mark.
Just like this, we weather the crisis.

for Y. L.

狷狂的一杯水

薄荷先生闭着眼，盘腿坐在角落。
雪飘下，一首诗已落成，
桌上的一杯水欲言又止。

他怕见这杯水过于四平八稳，
正如他怕见猥亵。
他爱满满的一杯——那正要
内溢四下，却又，外面般

欲言又止，忍在杯口的水，忍着，
如一个异想，大而无外，
忍住它高明而无形的翅膀。

因此，薄荷先生绝不会自外于自己，那
漫天大雪的自己，或自外于

被这蓝色角落轻轻牵扯的
来世，它伺者般端着我们
如杯子，那里面，水，总倾向于

多，总惶惑于少，而
这个少，这个少，这才是
我们唯一的溢满尘世的美满。

A Wildly Noble Glass of Water

Mr. Peppermint shuts his eyes, sits cross-legged in a corner.
Snow falling, a poem done,
a glass of water on the table wants to speak but swallows its words.

He is afraid to find this glass of water too stable and square
the way he is afraid to look at indecency.
He loves a glass filled to the brim—water about
to overflow, yet like its peripheral

wants to speak but swallows its words, enduring being in a glass, enduring,
like a fanciful idea, huge and boundless,
enduring its brilliant yet invisible wings.

So Mr. Peppermint would never stay beyond himself, the
self enveloped in falling snow, or beyond

an afterlife mildly involved with this blue
corner, subserviently it holds us with both hands
like a glass with water inside, always leaning toward

more, always perplexed by *less,* while
this *less,* this *less,* is in fact
our only bliss throughout this world of dust.

高窗

对面的高窗里，画眉鸟。
对面的稳密里，我看到了你。
对面的邈远里，或许你，是一个跟我
一模一样的人。是呀，或许你
就是我。

你或许也看到我在擦拭一张碟片如深井眼里的
白内障。是的，我在播放，但瞬刻间我又
退出了那部电影，虚空嘎地一响，画眉鸟
一惊。我哆嗦在红沙发上，
剥橙子。
我说，你在剥橙子呀，你说：
没错，我在剥橙子。我说：
瞧，世界又少了一颗橙子。
而你

把眉毛向北方扬起，把空衣架贴上玻璃窗，
把仙人掌挪到旋梯上拍照。
这时，长城外，

风沙乍起。这时，
你和我
几乎同时走到书桌前，拧亮灯，但
我们唯一的区别是：只有你，写下了
这首诗。

High Windows

In the high window across, a melodious laughing thrush.
In the trim density across, I see you.
In the distance across, perhaps you are exactly
like me. Oh yes, perhaps you
are me.

Perhaps you can also see me wiping clean a disc like a cataract
in the eye of a deep well. Yes, I'm broadcasting, but in an instant I'll
retreat from the film. The void creaks, the laughing thrush
startles. I shiver on a red sofa,
                                        peeling an orange.
I say, *You're peeling an orange.* You say,
Indeed, I'm peeling an orange. I say,
Look, one orange less in the world.
                                        But you

tilt your eyebrow to the north, hook a coat hanger to the glass window,
shift the cactus to a winding stair for a photo.
At this time, beyond the Great Wall,

a sandstorm breaks. At this time,
                                        you and I
walk nearly together to the desk, turn on the lamp, with
only one difference: you wrote down
this poem.

太平洋上，小岛国

是悠远缔造了这个岛，还是
这个岛泄露了悠远？午睡者裸卧
沙滩，身姿勾唤出一个奔波的问号：
他大汗淋漓，想挣脱北京的拥堵。

而岛上，正走着一位五光十色的
女酋长，慢镜头般走着，一边走，还一边
回望。她携带的悠远，如肩上的鹦鹉。
她说，她在等她的灵魂赶上来呢。

那鹦鹉说，这就是她走路的习惯。

In the Pacific Ocean, a Small Island Nation

Is it antiquity that founded this island, or
this island that exposed antiquity? He takes a nap, naked
on the beach, his posture evokes a scrambling question mark:
drenched in sweat, he wants to escape the congestion of Beijing.

On the island walks a flamboyant
sheikha, in slow motion—as she walks, she
looks back. She carries antiquity like a parrot on her shoulder.
She says she is waiting for her soul to catch up.

The parrot says this is how she always walks.

湘君

纽约的脆的薄荷味儿：我突然
想起长沙的一条飘飘的红领巾。
但你说你记不太清了。
我说，怎么，你真忘了，八O年你
你还替我改成了一条游泳裤呢。
你想了想，摇摇头，说，真忘了。
然后你深深地向咖啡杯底张望。

不过，你脸色一亮，说，我还记得去游泳，
那时湘江的水真是清得钻心。
“鱼翔浅底”，我说。“嗯”，你说。
那时你有志气，你又说，所以你帅，
所以你爱大吼出“临风骋望”的模样。
现在可真胖了，胖得……怎么说呢，
胖得有点见死不救了。

我们隔着桌子，忍着遥远。
哎，你说，你还记得
我们班的那个胖姐吗？她死了，好像是
骨癌。谁？我问。你说，就是那个黑里透红的，
叫沈仪的？
你摇摇我的手臂，好像我是死者。
你着急着说，哎，你怎么会想不起她呢？她还
教会你游蝶泳呢，你忘不了，她还三番五次
买“九嶷”牌香烟给你抽。

Goddess Xiang

The crisp mint scent of New York: I suddenly
recalled a Changsha red scarf in the wind.
But you said you couldn't really remember.
I said, *Why, you've forgotten, in 1980, you*
helped me alter a pair of swimming trunks.
You thought for a while, shook your head, and said, *Really, forgotten.*
Then you peered intensely into the bottom of a coffee cup.

But your face lit up and you said, *I do remember going for a swim.*
The water in the Xiang River was crystal clear.
Fish swim at ease in the shallows, I said. *Yup,* you replied.
You were ambitious, you added. *That was why you were handsome,*
enjoyed putting on thundering airs, as if "looking afar against the wind."
Now you've become so fat, such that . . . how should I put it,
such that you're beyond help.

Behind a table, we endured the distance.
Hey, you said. *Do you still remember*
that fat girl in our class? She died. Probably from
bone cancer. Who, I asked. You responded, *The rosy one.*
Wasn't her name Shen Yi?
You shook my arm as if I were dead.
You panicked. *Hey, why can't you remember her? She*
taught you the butterfly stroke. You can't have forgotten. She kept
buying you Jiuyi cigarettes.

哪个胖姐？哪个？我在你脸上搜找着。
我印象里怎么完全没有这个人呢？
我着急地问，我着急地望着
咖啡杯底那些迭起如歌的漩涡，

那些浩大烟波里从善如流的死者。

2004

Which fat girl? Which one? I searched your face.
How could this person vanish from my memory?
I anxiously asked and anxiously gazed
at the whirlpool at the bottom of the coffee cup,

dead souls flowing from foggy tidal waves.

2004

看不见的鸦片战争

宫廷后院。一棵铁树开着花，但谁都只对皇上
谈月牙儿。太监照常耳语，用漂亮的句法说
没有的事。他最爱用“小雀儿”这个词儿。
比如皇上问那守南疆炮台的武将这阵子如何，
他答曰：“那小雀儿还行，不过……”，他

险些儿说了出来，要不是他偶尔碰着裤兜里的
玉环，这些天他都用长指甲在里面把玩
这小礼品。
　　　　　南风袭面，而云朵不断陈列着异像：
有时是个技工模样的人，蹲着摆弄着什么；
有时是一个大胡子的半身像（有点像马克思），
肃穆地飘过；
有时是一个耸肩摊手的女人，像在说：“啊，我？
　　我？我会在维多利亚时代撒这样的谎？”

他琢磨望天的皇上是在看自己看到的东西还是
别的。是的，皇上在看一个小胖婴孩，
咿咿呀呀地敲着奶瓶，他突然扬起眉，
　　樱桃小口伶俐地说：
“来，叫我一声亲爹，我就把闹钟给你！”

有一瞬，皇上真伸开五指想抓住什么，但他
转眼又在龙椅睡了，睁着一只眼，双拳半坠；

The Invisible Opium War

Imperial backyard. A sago palm blossoms, yet everyone speaks only of
the crescent
moon to the Emperor. The eunuch whispers as usual, speaking of the
nonexistent
in lovely syntax. His favorite words are *little sparrow.*
For instance, when the Emperor asks about the general in charge of an
artillery battery in southern Xinjiang,
he replies, *That little sparrow is doing fine, but . . .* He

nearly spills it all, if not for the jade ring he feels in his trouser pocket now
and then; these days he keeps playing with his long fingernails in it with
this small gift.
The south wind rushes into the face as clouds display visions nonstop:
sometimes a man who looks like a mechanic, squatting and fiddling with
something;
sometimes a full-bearded bust (slightly resembling Marx),
drifting past solemnly;
sometimes a woman who shrugs and waves her hands, as if saying, *Ah, me?*
Me? Would I tell such lies in the Victorian era?

He mulls over the Emperor looking at the sky. *Is he looking at what he can see or*
something else? Yes, the Emperor is looking at a fat baby
yi-yi-ya-ya-ing while it knocks on a milk bottle. Suddenly his eyebrows rise,
and with petite cherry lips he says astutely,
Come, call me Daddy, and I'll give you an alarm clock!

In an instant, the Emperor stretches his fingers out to grab something, but
in a flash falls asleep again on the throne, one eye open, fists half drooping;

这时，假如你碰巧从云中
往下看，一定能证实大地满是难言的图案。

at this moment, if you happen to look down
from the clouds, you will no doubt confirm that the earth is full of patterns
beyond words.

灯笼镇

灯笼镇，灯笼镇
你，像最新的假消息
谁都不想要你
除非你自设一个雕像

（合唱）
假雕像，一座雕像
灯红酒绿

（画外声）
搁在哪里，搁在哪里

老虎衔起了雕像
朝最后的林中逝去

雕像披着黄昏
像披着自己的肺腑

灯笼镇，灯笼镇，不想呼吸

2010. 1. 13 图宾根

Lantern Town

lantern town, lantern town
you—like the latest fake news
nobody wants you
unless you build your own statue

(Chorus)
fake statue, a statue
extravagant decadence

(Voice-over)
where can it go, where can it go

a tiger holds the statue in its mouth
and fades into the last of the woods

the statue is draped in dusk
like in its internal organs

lantern town, lantern town, I don't want to breathe

January 13, 2010—Tübingen

Bygones

I first met Zhang Zao in the early spring of 1985. Together with the poet Peng Yanjiao and Ma Gaoming, we were preparing a magazine for poetry in translation, *International Poetry Scene*, and discussing the possibility of its publication by Chongqing Publishing House. It was an unforgettable time for me, meeting young poets like Bai Hua, who wrote about our meeting in his memoir, *Left* (2009). Zhang Zao was only twenty-three—a graduate of the Sichuan International Studies University, slim and agile. I recall being struck by his brilliant talent in the poems he showed me, such as "Mirror" and "Who Art Thou." About a year later, he left for Germany. Prior to his departure, when he came to Beijing to take care of some paperwork, my friends and I hosted him.

In the summer of 1989, I spent four months in Berlin and made a special trip to Trier University, where Zhang Zao was pursuing his PhD. He felt very lonely and so did I. Shortly after the overseas revival of our literary journal *Jintian*, I invited him to serve as its poetry editor. Zhang edited the journal's poetry for over a decade, publishing work by many renowned poets and introducing new talent to *Jintian*, before stepping down. His editorial contributions were significant.

The other *Jintian* poetry editor, Song Lin, resided in Paris. I first moved to Denmark, then Holland. As we weren't that far from one another, we frequently got together. During one particularly memorable editorial meeting in a mill-converted villa near Trier, we met the German woman who owned the villa and a Russian couple who taught voice. That night, we drank a lot of red wine and even frightened them with our rowdy Russian folk songs and revolutionary songs.

Later, Zhang Zao received his PhD and became a professor at the University of Tübingen. In the summer of 1995, I brought along my parents and daughter to spend some time with Zhang. He was very good with elderly people and children. With a recording of Isaac Stern playing violin,

Zhang Zao became my daughter's first music teacher. She has kept the record to this day.

Zhang Zao's proficiency in German and English was impressive, but he was never able to adapt to the loneliness of a life abroad. It was a test, he said, that poets and writers must go through. He also never got used to European cuisine. Each time we visited, he served dishes like Hunan-cured meat with a generous portion of chili. We also frequented the local Chinese restaurants. Once, with a friend he even went out of his way to drive me to a nice restaurant in Luxembourg for dinner. Zhang indulged himself in beer and cigarettes, and never failed to end up half drunk.

We last met in the spring of 2004 while I was participating in a series of poetry-related events in Berlin. When I brought my wife to visit Zhang in Tübingen, we were shocked to see his son kicking a soccer ball against his audio equipment in a disheveled apartment. Zhang Zao's personal life was in no better shape: he'd lost his job and his relationship was in crisis.

In the late nineties, Zhang Zao began returning to China on a regular basis. Whenever back, he would always phone me in a state of overexcitement. Around 2006, he was faced with the dilemma of "homecoming," whether to move back to China for good. We exchanged several lengthy phone conversations. I knew very well the weaknesses in his character; the sensual pleasures in life, coupled with mainland China's fickle environment, would ruin him.

"If you return to the mainland," I said, "you'll end up giving up poetry." Zhang agreed. But he could no longer stand the loneliness abroad.

After his move to Beijing, we phoned each other a few times but soon realized we had less and less to share. Gradually we lost contact. I would occasionally hear of his whereabouts from friends. Then in December of 2009, Bai Hua informed me of Zhang Zao's cancer diagnosis. I was shocked and emailed Zhang immediately. He responded briefly, ending the note with *I will persevere.*

Zhang Zao is undoubtedly a prodigy of Chinese contemporary poetry. His linguistic sensibility is like a disease. He wrote numerous radical and experimental poems; some succeeded, some failed. Nevertheless, his contributions to Chinese modern poetry are extraordinary. He possessed both a thorough grasp of European literature and culture and an introspective understanding of the broad, profound range of Asian aesthetics: between these two philosophies, he sought a new tension and melting point.

Bei Dao
Translated from the Chinese by Fiona Sze-Lorrain

Notes

Mirror
The title literally translates as "In the Mirror."

Autumn Drama
According to the poet Bai Hua, each section is a narrative about a specific person in Zhang Zao's life:
Section IV refers to Zhang's first love;
Section V is addressed to a former girlfriend;
Section VI speaks of Zhang's friendship with Bai Hua;
Section VII refers to a Russian-American professor who taught Zhang Zao Anglo-American literature at Sichuan International Studies University in the 1980s.

Late Autumn Story
Jiangnan—literally translated as *river* and *south*—refers to the region south of the lower Yangtze River. Jiangnan's cities include Nanjing, Hangzhou, Shanghai, Suzhou, Wuxi, and Yangzhou.

The Blissful Corduroy Dance
"An educated man is not a pot" is a Confucian saying translated by Simon Leys. It means an educated person is not a tool meant just for one purpose or use. Leys's translation is from his *An Educated Man Is Not a Pot: On the University* (Melbourne: Black Inc. Books, 2017).

The Prince of Chu Dreams of Rain
The Prince of Chu may refer either to King Huai—the sovereign of Chu who reigned from 328 to 299 BCE—or King Qingxiang who ruled the state of Chu from 298 to 263 BCE.

Early Spring, February

"A hidden dragon waits for action" is a Chinese idiom that cautions against haste, particularly when time is not yet ripe for action.

Memories of Mount Lu

Mount Lu refers to Mount Yuelu in Changsha, Hunan province.

Love and Death of a German Spy in the England of a Sweet Nightingale [a lyric sequence]

The opening quotation is from John Keats's poem "Ode to a Nightingale" (1819).

Schermanski the German Soldier's Death Sentence

The poem contains the following Russian phrases:
Kakaya sevodnya khoroshaya pogoda! ["What fine weather today!"]
Ya tebya lyublyu! ["I love you"]

It also contains the following German phrases [translated by Jan Wagner]:
Jawohl ["Yes"]
Ich liebe dich ["I love you"]
Bitte, bitte, Gnade! ["Please, please, have mercy!"]
Du bist nicht verloren! ["You are not lost!"]
Lebewohl! ["Goodbye!"]

Kafka to Felice

Franz Kafka was twice engaged to Felice Bauer (1887–1960)—first in April 1914 and again in July 1917. Both engagements lasted only a few months. For more information about Kafka's letters to Bauer, I recommend *Letters to Felice,* first published by Schocken Books in 1967, edited by Erich Heller and Jurgen Born, translated from the German by James Stern and Elisabeth Duckworth.

I have sought clarification from German poet, translator, and literary critic Jan Wagner, who has translated the opening quotation by Kafka as "Again nothing today, beloved, sad." However, Wagner points out to me that this too seems to be a misquote; in Kafka's letters to Felice Bauer, he has found this instead: *Liebste, heute wieder nichts, traurig*. ["Beloved, again nothing today, sad."] According to Wagner, that is from a postcard dated October 10, 1916, sent from Prague. By this, Kafka meant that again, no letter from Felice had arrived.

Talisman

In stanza one, line five, the phrase "thrust a fist with sandalwood oil" implies thrusting a fist "in a smooth way," that is, "to conquer force with gentleness."

According to the manuscript version preserved by poets Chen Dongdong and Bai Hua, the title of this poem and the word *talisman* recurring throughout the poem were first substituted by *mascot*. In Zhang Zao's poetry collection *Letters in Four Seasons* (Beijing: Culture and Art Publishing House, 1998), the poem was retitled "Talisman" and dated 1992.

The Lark This Year

This poem alludes to a verse "嘤其鸣矣，求其友声。" ["'Ying' they cry, / Each searching its mate's voice."] from "The Woodman's Axe (165)," one of the "Minor Odes" in the Confucian classic *The Book of Songs* (*Shijing*):

> *Ding, ding* goes the woodman's axe;
> *Ying, ying* cry the birds,
> Leave the dark valley,
> Mount to the high tree.
> "Ying" they cry,
> Each searching its mate's voice.

[From *The Book of Songs (Shijing)*. Trans. Arthur Waley. Edited with additional translations by Joseph R. Allen. New York: Grove Press, 1996. 137.]

Instead of the verb *sing*, Zhang Zao uses *knock* in this poem to evoke his yearning for a soulmate.

Grandpa

Wang Lun is a close friend of the Tang poet Li Po. In his poem "To Wang Lun," Li Po spoke highly of Wang Lun's friendship:

> Peach Blossom Lake
> is a thousand feet deep
>
> but it can't compare
> with Wang Lun's love
> or the way he said
> goodbye

[From *Five T'ang Poets: Wang Wei, Li Po, Tu Fu, Li Ho, Li Shang-yin*. Trans. David Young. Oberlin: Oberlin College Press/FIELD Translation Series 15, 1990. 65.]

Dialogue with Tsvetaeva [a sequence of sonnets]

The opening quotation is from Marina Tsvetaeva's prose piece "*Le Chinois*," first published in Paris in a Russian daily newspaper, *Poslednie novosti* (*Les Dernières Nouvelles*) on October 24, 1934. See Tsvetaeva, Marina. *Assurance sur la Vie/Le Chinois*. Trans. Véronique Lossky. Sauve: Clémence Hiver, 1991. 8 and 21.

2

The phrase "eternal sorrow" is from the last verse of a well-known poem by Tang poet Li Po, "Bringing in the Wine" (*Jiang jin jiu* 将进酒).

8
The correct version of the opening quotation should be "*Wenn Du mich wirklich sehen willst, so musst Du handeln*!" This is translated by Jan Wagner as "If you really want to see me, you have to act!" And Wagner mentions that while this citation makes sense, this remains a misquote.

The correct line is from Tsvetaeva's letter [August 22, 1926] to Rainer Maria Rilke: "*Rainer, ganz ernst: wenn Du mich wirklich, mit Augen, sehen willst, mußt Du handeln, d.h. — 'In zwei Wochen bin ich da und da. Ob Du kommst?' Das muß von Dir kommen. Wie das Datum.*" In Wagner's translation: "Rainer, seriously: if you really, with your eyes, want to see me, you have to act, that is—'In two weeks I'll be there and there. Will you come?' That has to come from you. Just like the date."

12
"Katyusha" (1938) is a Russian folk song composed by Matvey Blanter (1903–1990). It was a popular song during the Second World War.

Nightview, New York
The opening quotation is from the third stanza of Walt Whitman's "Song of Myself" in his *Leaves of Grass* (1855).

West Lake Dream
West Lake is a famous lake in Hangzhou, Zhejiang province, known for its scenic beauty and cultural history.

Clouds
This lyric sequence carries a dedication in German, "to Zhang Deng for his second birthday" [in Jan Wagner's translation].

Zhang Deng is Zhang Zao's eldest son.

6
The foot *chi* refers to a Chinese foot, a traditional unit of measurement equivalent to a third of a meter (33 $^{1}/_{3}$ cm).

Letters in Four Seasons
The two characters 春秋 are literally translated as "spring autumn." They also mean an entire year (four seasons), one's age, or time in general. Additionally, the term may refer to Confucius's *Spring and Autumn Annals* or the historical Spring and Autumn period (770–476 BCE).

Earth Song
Located in central Shanghai, Nanjing Road is the most famous commercial street in Shanghai.

Located in the Huangpu district, Huangpu Park is the oldest public park in Shanghai. It first opened in 1868.

Oriental Pearl Tower is a television and radio tower that stands at a height of 468 meters across the Bund in Shanghai.

Off to Jiangnan
See the note on Jiangnan under "Late Autumn Story."

This poem carries a dedication with a phrase in German, "for Zhong Ming, dear friend of many distances" [in Jan Wagner's translation].

Song of a Wall Driller and the Ultimate Ear
The phrase *mon semblable* can be found in the last verse of French poet Charles Baudelaire's poem, "Au Lecteur" ("To the Reader") from *Les Fleurs du Mal* (*The Flowers of Evil*) (1857): "*— Hypocrite lecteur, — mon semblable, — mon frère !*"

Robert Lowell translated *mon semblable* as "my double," while Richard Howard translated it as "my alias."

See Baudelaire, Charles. "To the Reader." *Flowers of Evil: A Selection*. Trans. Robert Lowell. Eds. Jackson Mathews and Marthiel Mathews. New York: New Directions, 1955. 5.

Also see Baudelaire, Charles. "To the Reader." *Les Fleurs du Mal*. Trans. Richard Howard. New Hampshire: David R. Godine, 1982. 6.

Drunken Song
The word *chicken* for the phrase "eat chicken" in line eleven also refers to a prostitute.

Emperor Qin, also known as Ying Zheng, Qin Shi Huang, or the first Emperor of China, unified China and ruled the Qin dynasty from 221 to 210 BCE. The assassin refers to Jing Ke, who was sent by Crown Prince Dan from the state of Yan to assassinate King Ying Zheng in 227 BCE. Jing Ke failed and was killed by King Ying Zheng's warrior guards.

Adieu Schloss Solitude
Schloss Solitude, also known as Castle Solitude or Solitude Palace, is a late-Baroque palace in Stuttgart, Germany. Built between 1763 and 1775, it served as Duke Carl Eugen von Württemberg's summer retreat and hunting residence.

Father
A long, narrow island in the middle of the Xiang River, Orange Isle is one of the top scenic spots of Changsha in Hunan province.

High Windows
This poem likely alludes to British poet Philip Larkin's "High Windows" (1967).

Goddess Xiang

Goddess Xiang refers to Zhang Zao's girlfriend, the "you" in this poem.

One of the "Nine Songs" (*Jiu ge* 九歌) by Qu Yuan, the famous ancient Chinese poet from the state of Chu during the Warring States era, is addressed to Goddess Xiang. For more information, I recommend *The Songs of the South: An Ancient Chinese Anthology of Poems by Qu Yuan and Other Poets*. Trans. David Hawkes. London: Penguin Classics, 2011. 104–107.

The Invisible Opium War

This poem was initially meant to be the first of a sequence. Zhang's original manuscript version contains a numbered heading *One*.

Lantern Town

This last poem was written about two months before Zhang Zao's death. Due to Zhang's deteriorating health, several of its Chinese characters are not particularly legible. They were deciphered and edited by the poet's close friends before the poem was published in his posthumous collection, *Poems by Zhang Zao* (Beijing: People's Literature Publishing House, 2010).

About the Author and Translator

Zhang Zao 张枣 is a key literary figure of the "third generation" of Chinese contemporary poetry. Born in 1962 in Changsha, Hunan province, he rose to national fame as one of the "Five Sichuan Masters." Greatly admired by his peers for championing a complex yet harmonizing fusion of traditional writing and avant-garde flair in his work, and for his versatility in many foreign languages, Zhang was a recognized literary critic, translator, and scholar. In 1986, he moved to Germany. For several years, he served as poetry editor for the literary magazine *Jintian* and taught at the University of Tübingen. He returned briefly to China in 2004 and lectured at Henan University the next spring. In 2007, he began teaching in Beijing at the Minzu University of China. Zhang Zao died in 2010 in Tübingen, the town of Hölderlin. He was forty-seven.

Fiona Sze-Lorrain is a writer, poet, translator, musician, and editor who writes and translates in English, French, and Chinese. She is the author of a novel in stories *Dear Chrysanthemums* (Scribner, 2023), five poetry collections including *Rain in Plural* (Princeton, 2020) and *The Ruined Elegance* (Princeton, 2016), and fifteen books of translation, most recently *Moonlight Rests on My Left Palm* by Yu Xiuhua (Astra House, 2021). Longlisted for the 2024 Andrew Carnegie Medal for Excellence in Fiction and the PEN Award for Poetry in Translation, she was a finalist for the Los Angeles Times Book Prize, the Derek Walcott Prize for Poetry, and the Best Translated Book Award. She is a judge for the 2025 International Dublin Literary Award. As a zheng harpist, she has performed around the world. She lives in Paris.

JINTIAN SERIES

Flash Cards / Yu Jian
Translated by Wang Ping & Ron Padgett
ISBN 978-0-9815521-5-6

The Changing Room / Zhai Yongming
Translated by Andrea Lingenfelter
ISBN 978-0-9815521-3-2

Doubled Shadows / Ouyang Jianghe
Translated by Austin Woerner
ISBN 978-0-9815521-7-0

A Phone Call from Dalian / Han Dong
Edited by Nicky Harman
Translated by Nicky Harman, Maghiel van Crevel,
Yu Yan Chen, Naikan Tao, Tony Prince & Michael Day
ISBN 978-0-9832970-1-7

Wind Says / Bai Hua
Translated by Fiona Sze-Lorrain
ISBN 978-0-9832970-6-2

I Can Almost See the Clouds of Dust / Yu Xiang
Translated by Fiona Sze-Lorrain
ISBN 978-0-9832970-9-3

Canyon in the Body / Lan Lan
Translated by Fiona Sze-Lorrain
ISBN 978-1-938890-01-7

Something Crosses My Mind / Wang Xiaoni
Translated by Eleanor Goodman
ISBN 978-1-938890-06-2

Sunday Sparrows / Song Lin
Translated by Jami Proctor-Xu
ISBN 978-1-938890-25-3

October Dedications / Mang Ke
Translated by Lucas Klein,
Huang Yibing & Jonathan Stalling
ISBN 978-1-938890-08-6

Floral Mutter / Ya Shi
Translated by Nick Admussen
ISBN 978-1-938890-89-5

Mirror / Zhang Zao
Translated by Fiona Sze-Lorrain
ISBN 978-1-938890-35-2